DINOSAUR

Coloring Book

Belong to

___

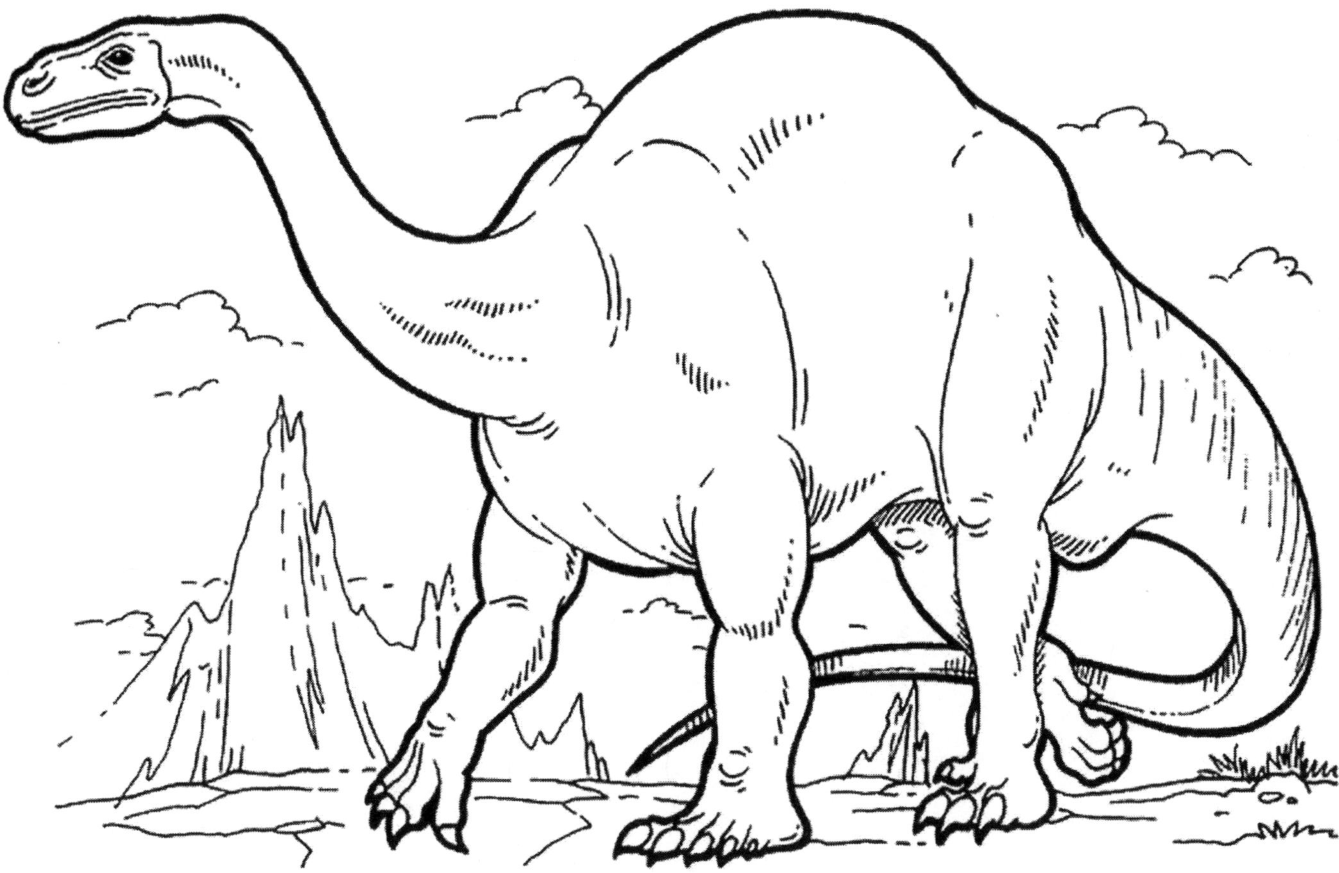

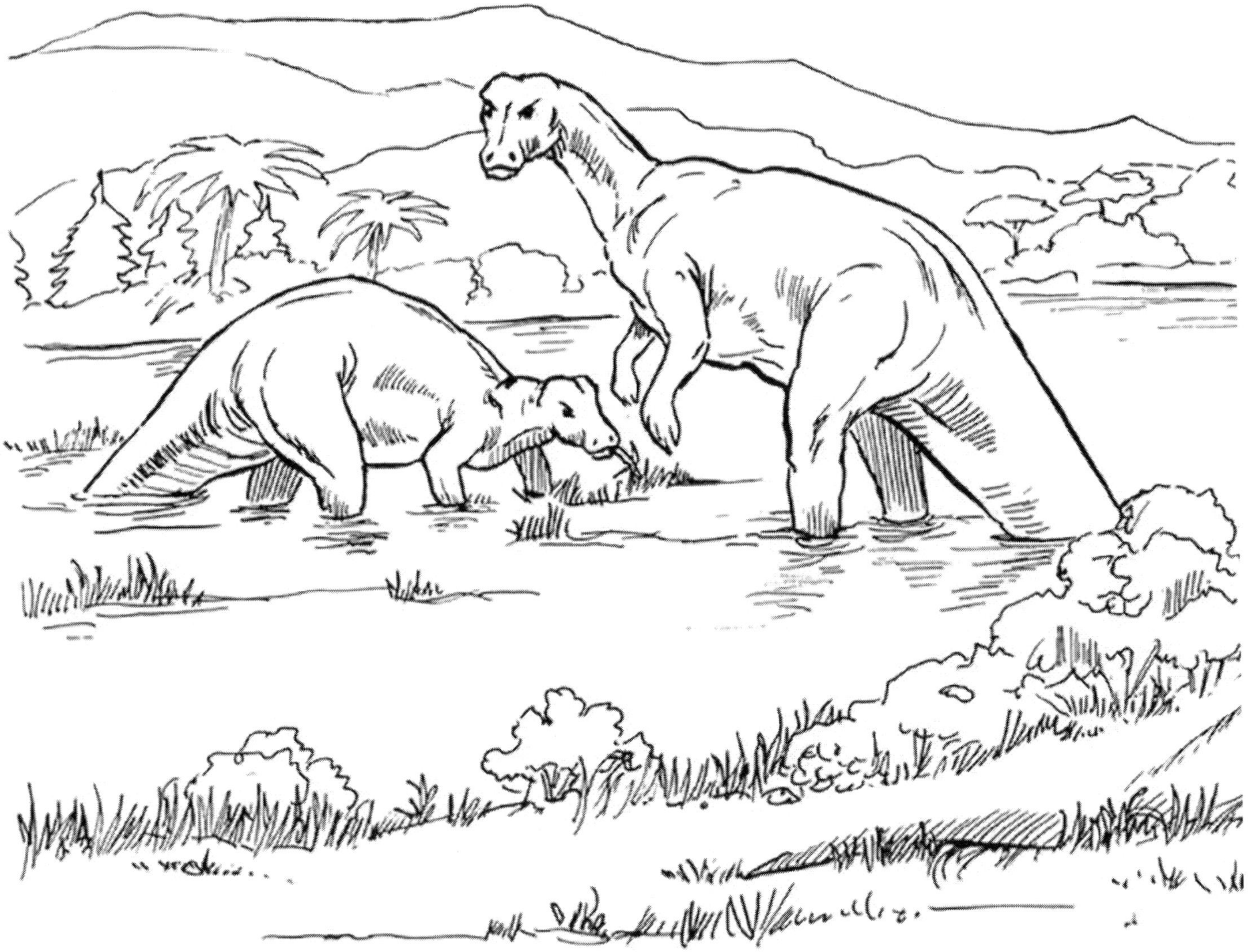

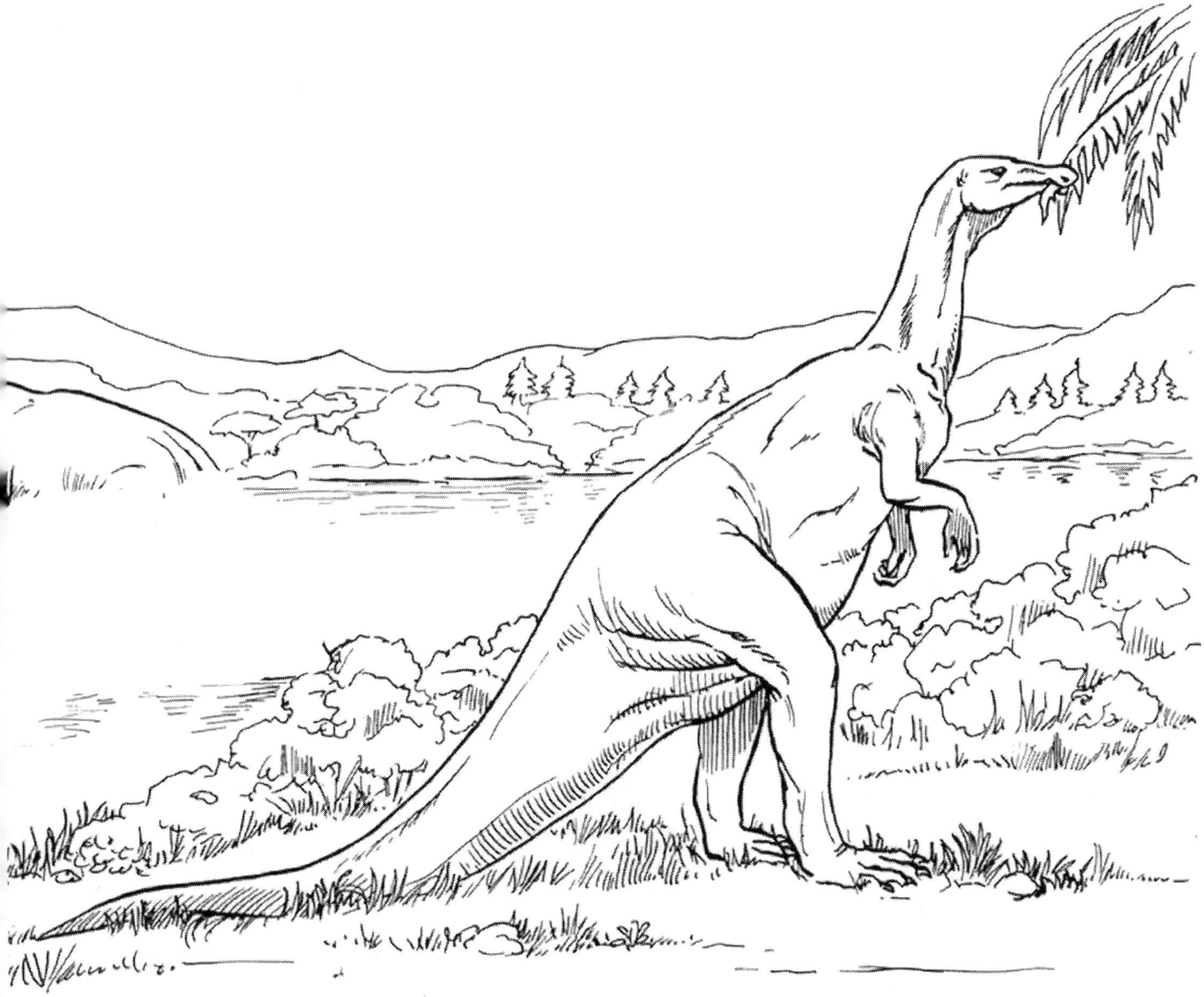

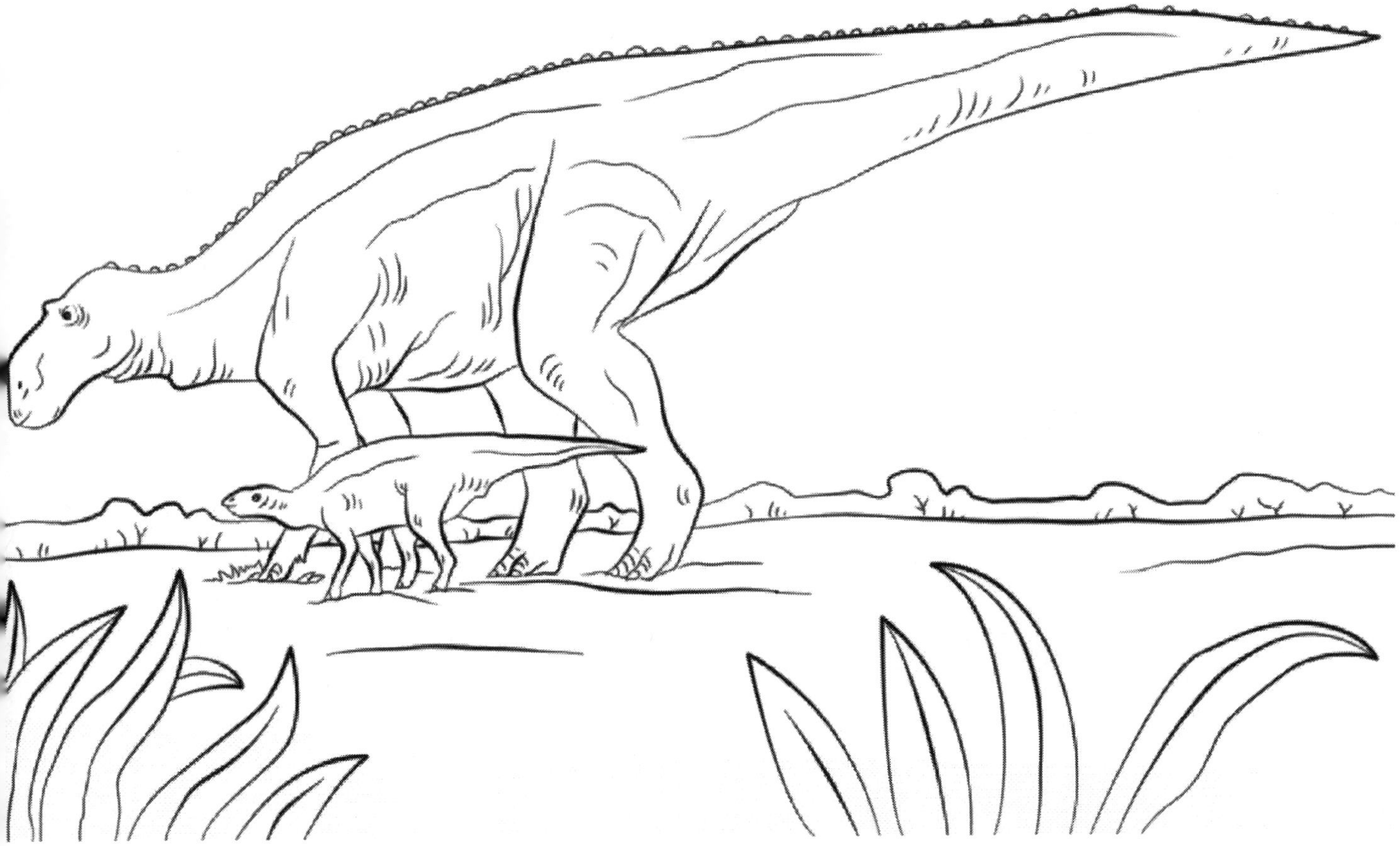

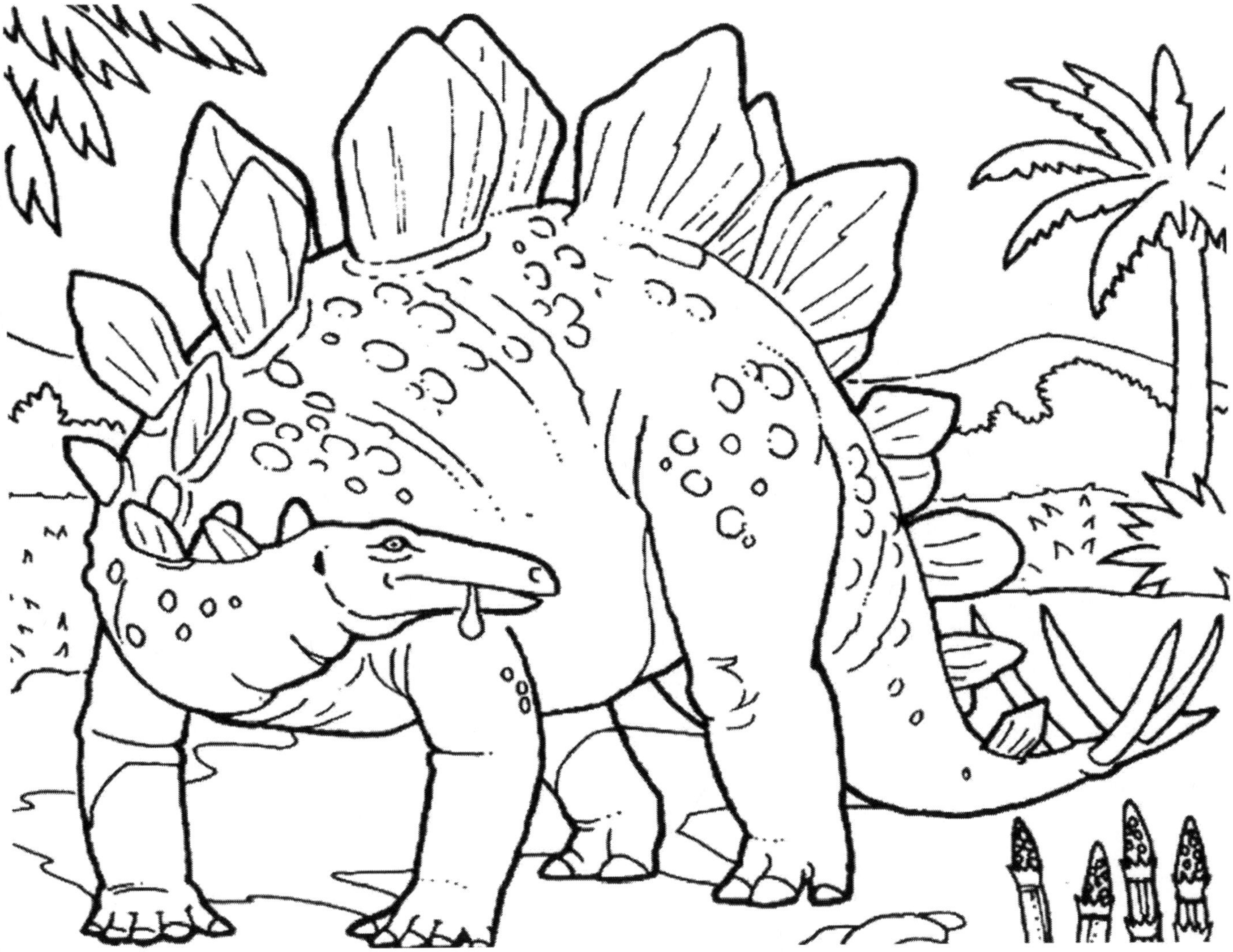

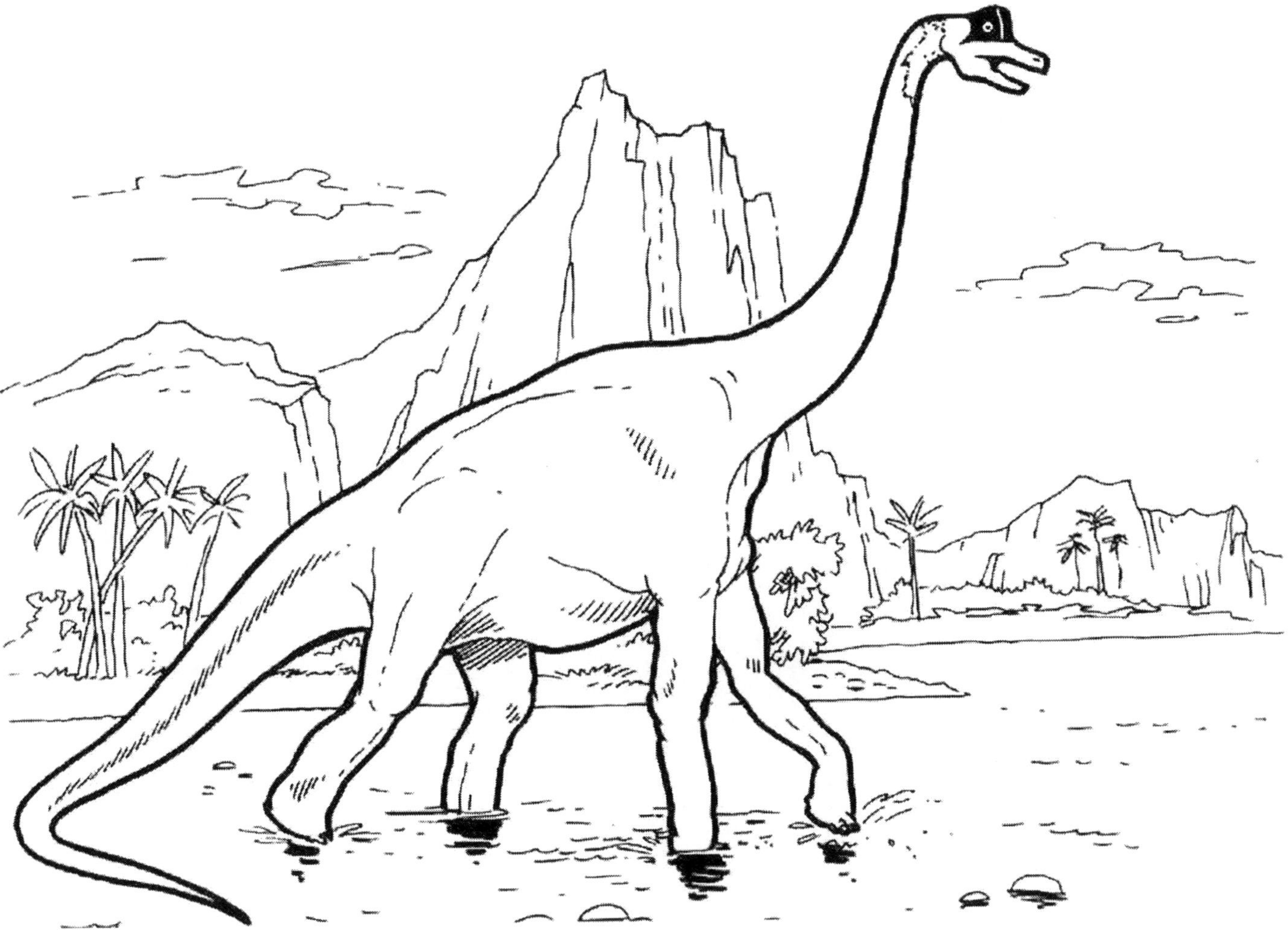

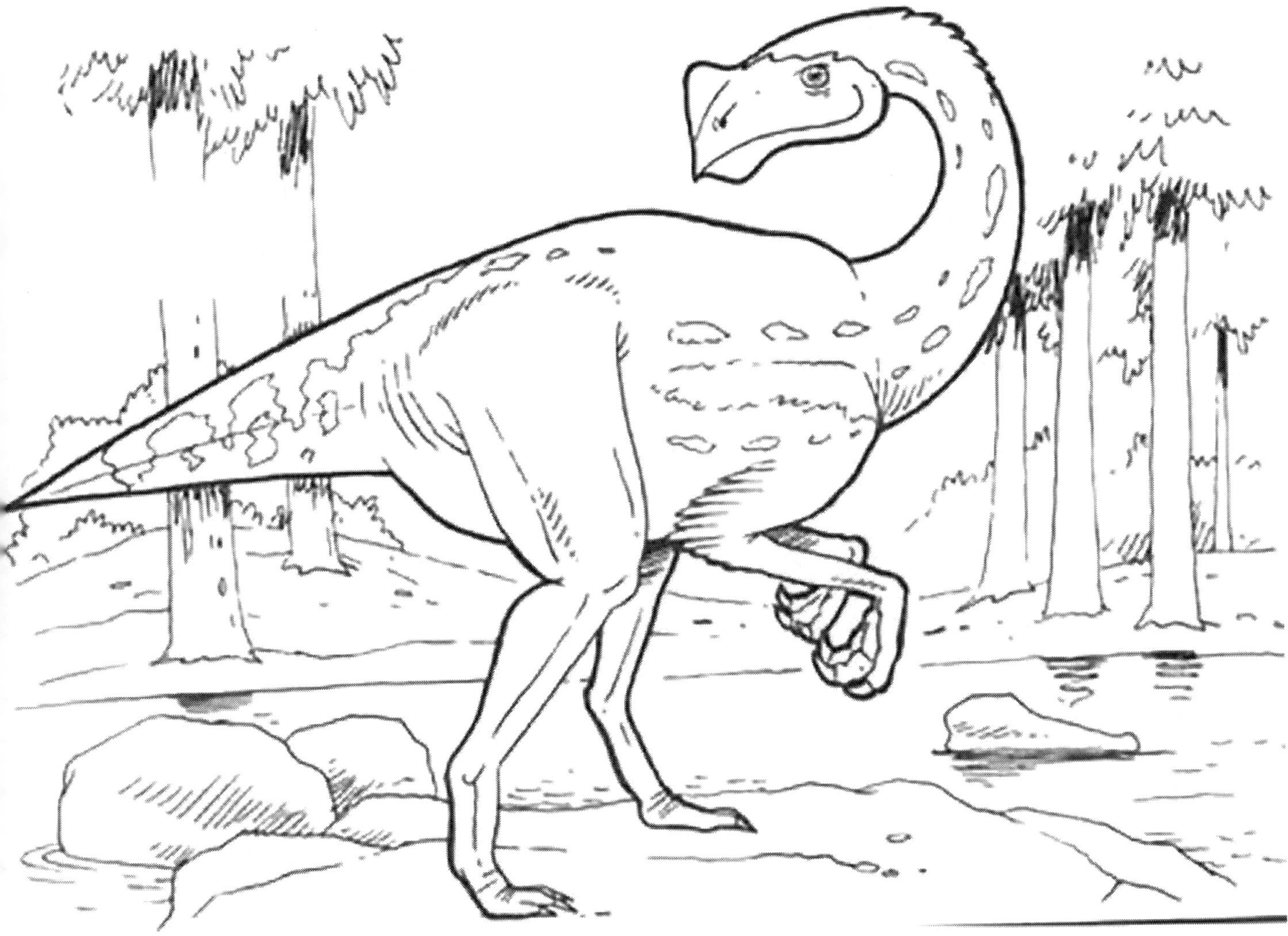

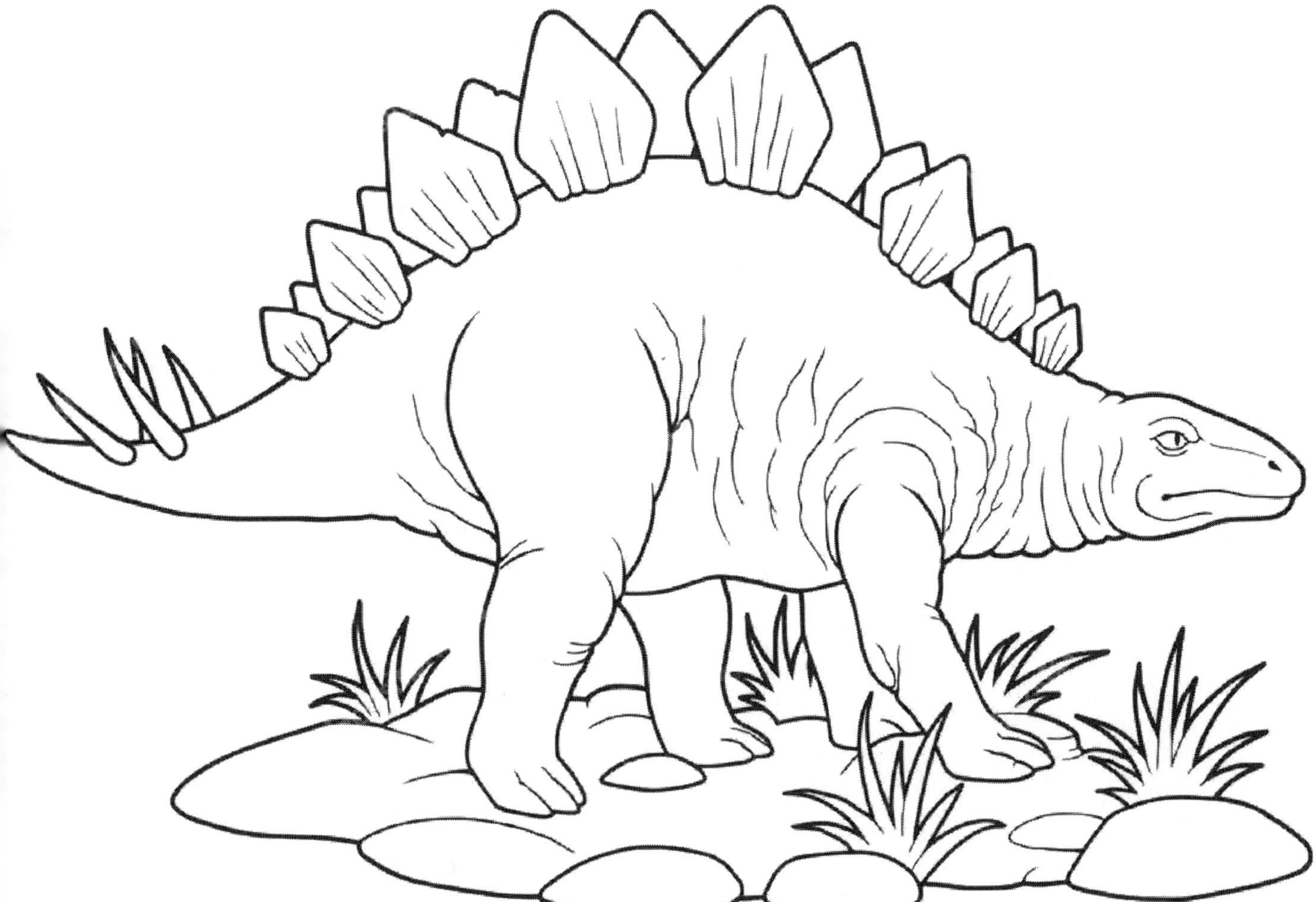

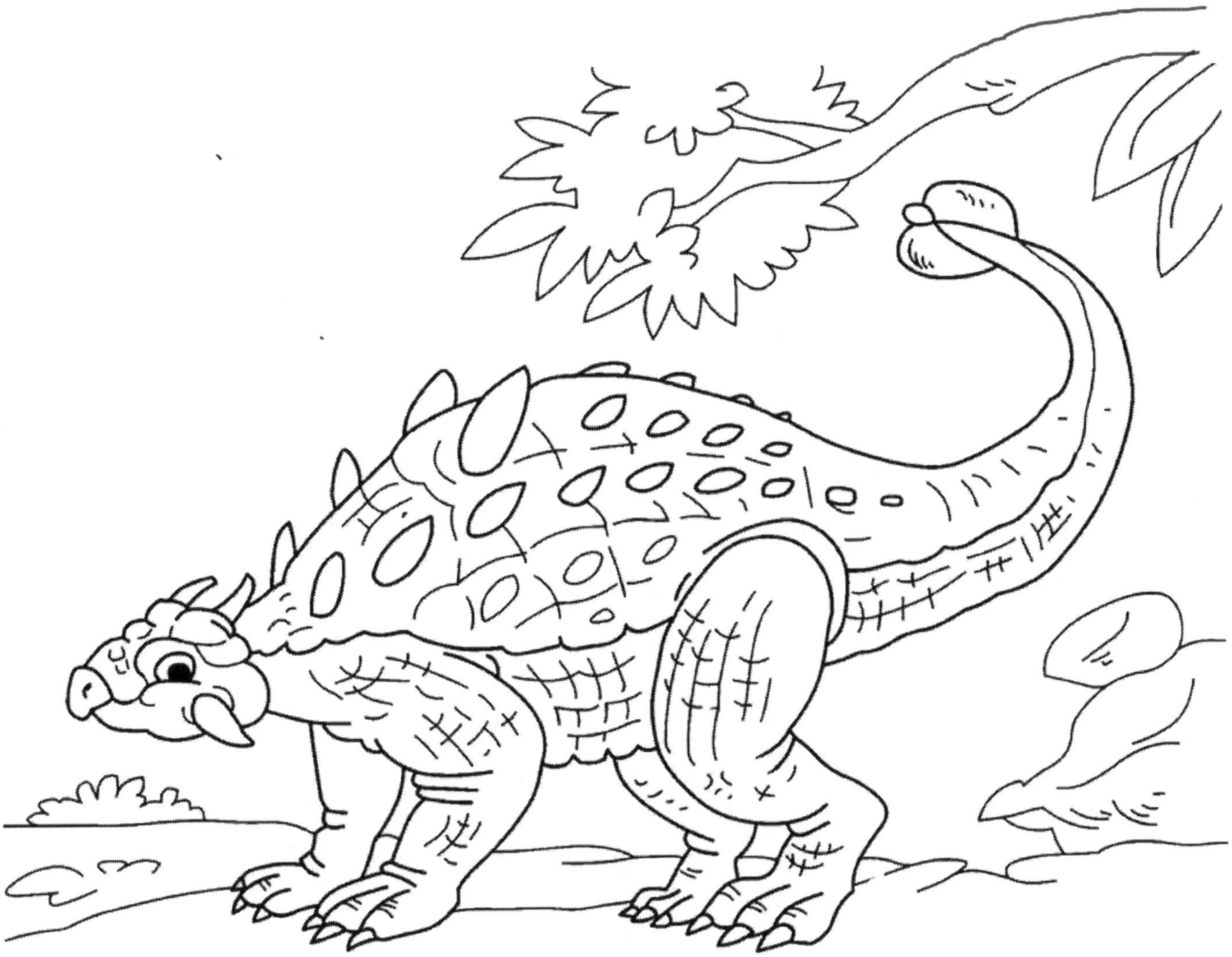

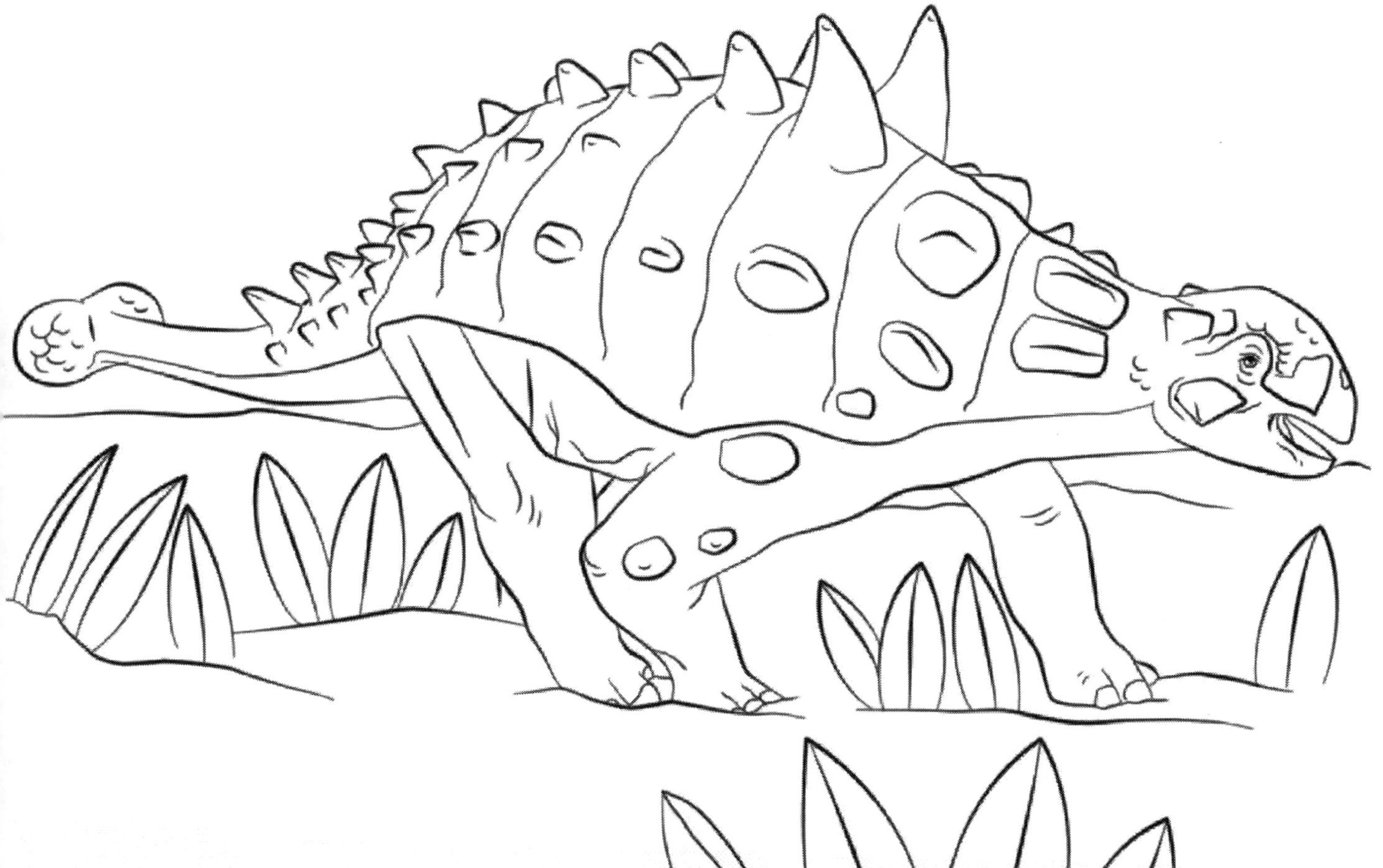

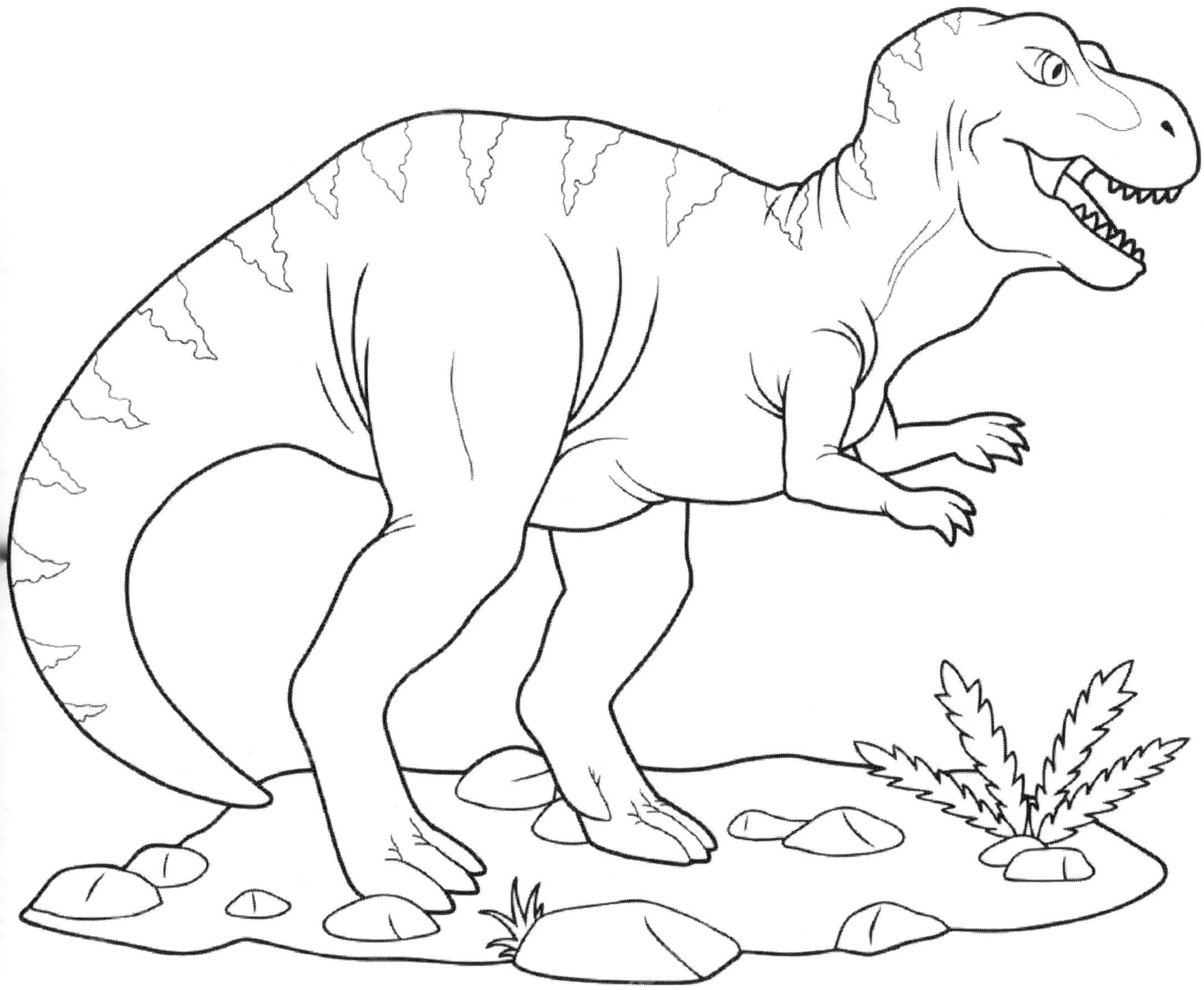

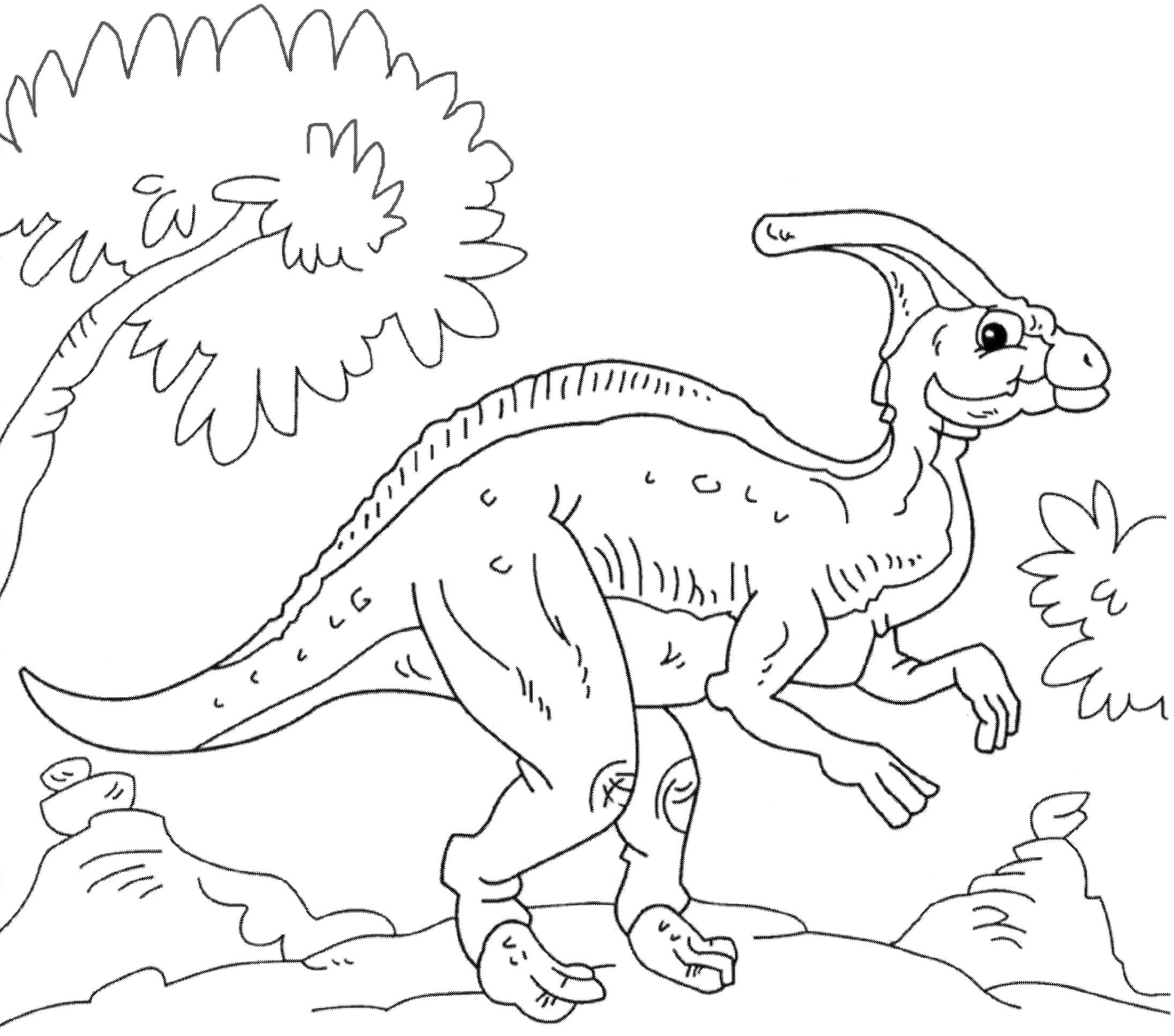

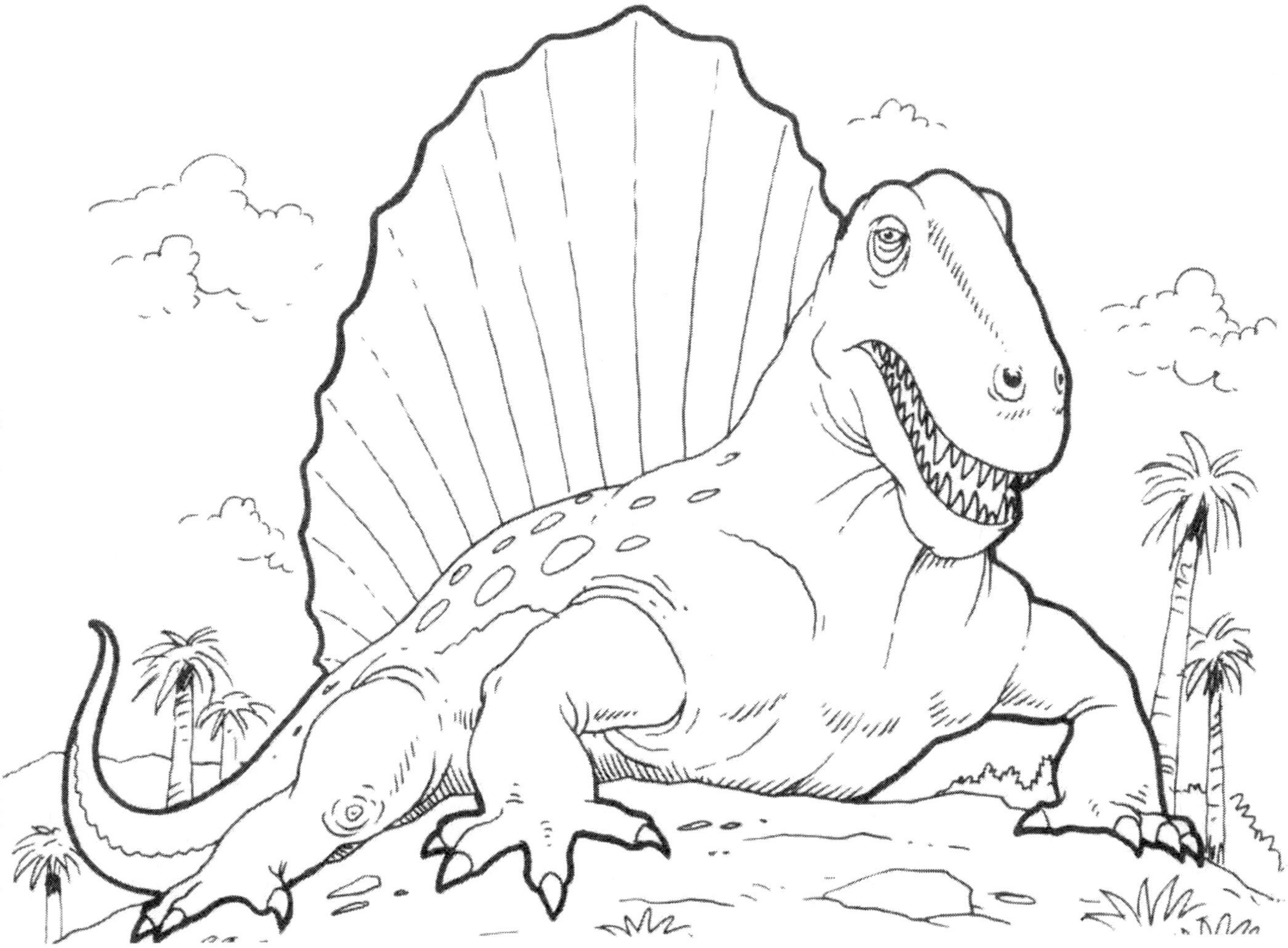

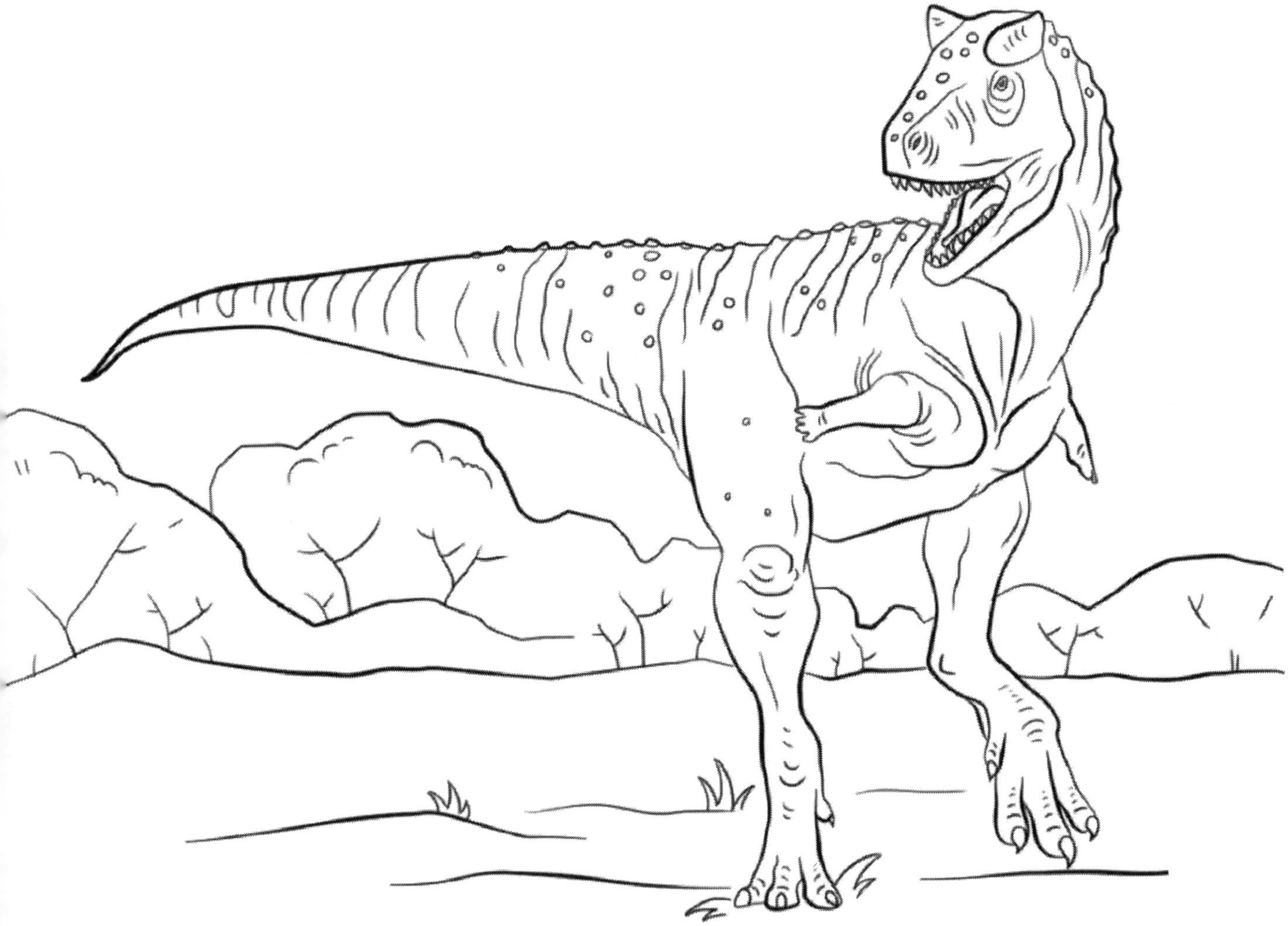

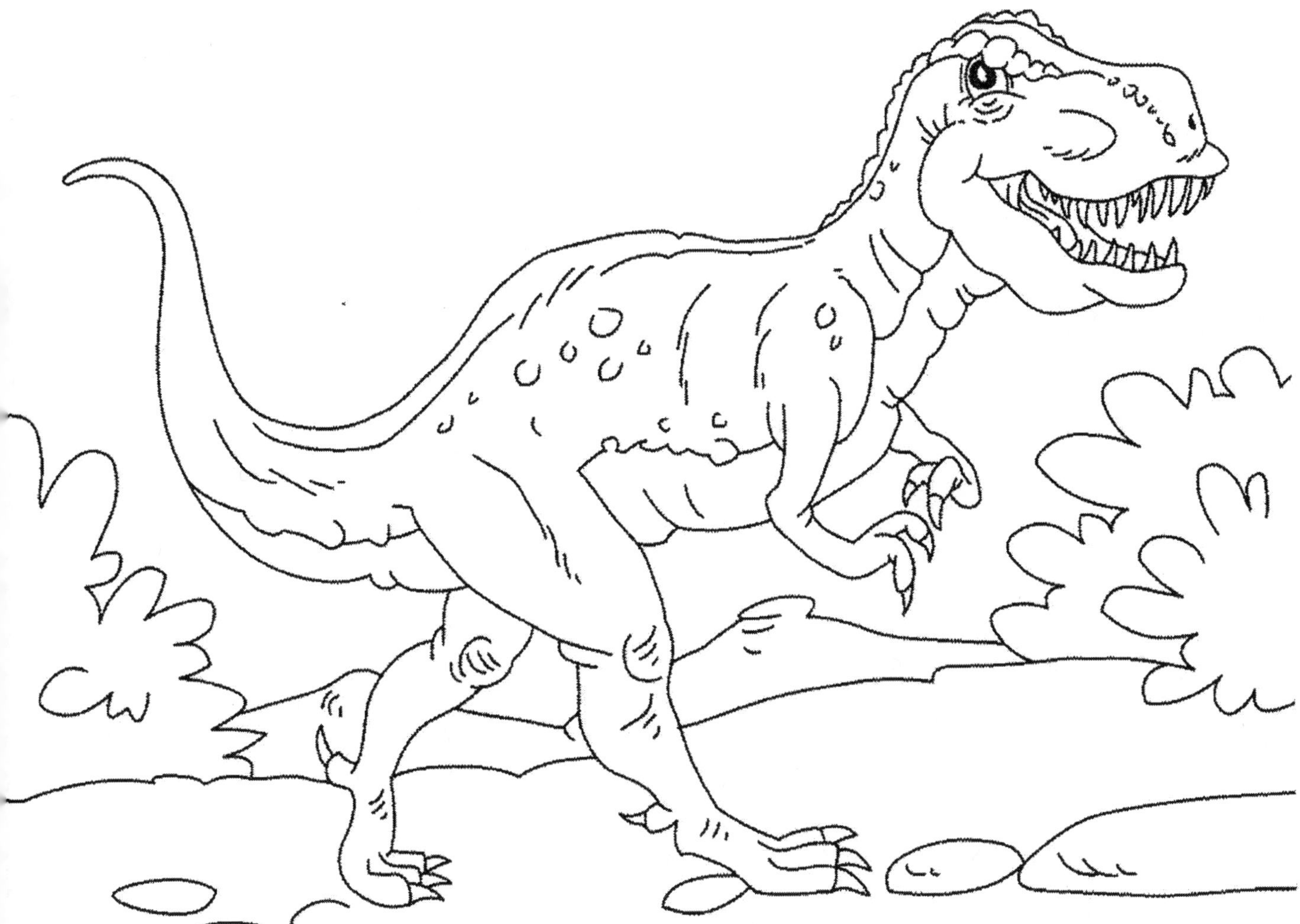

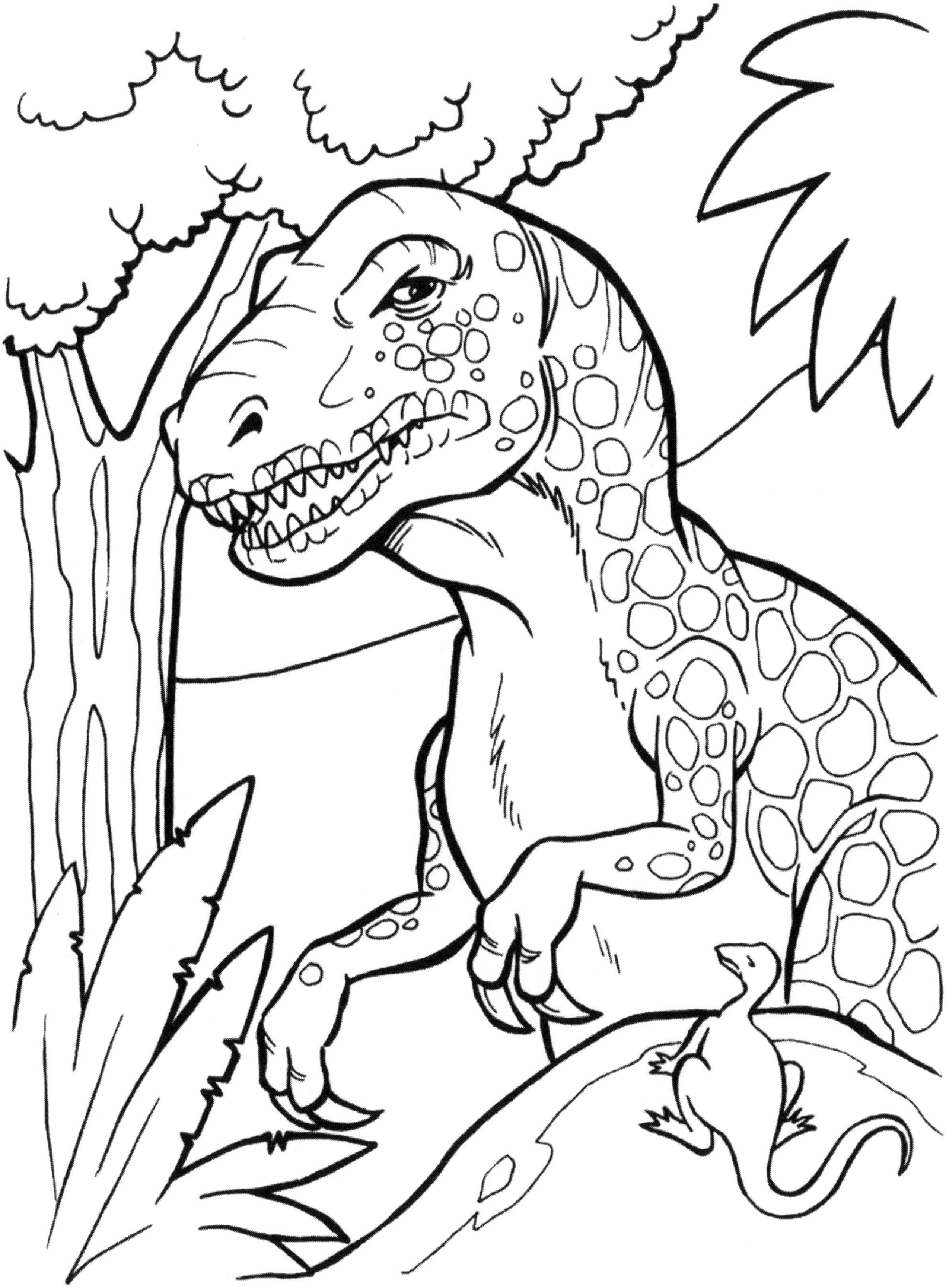

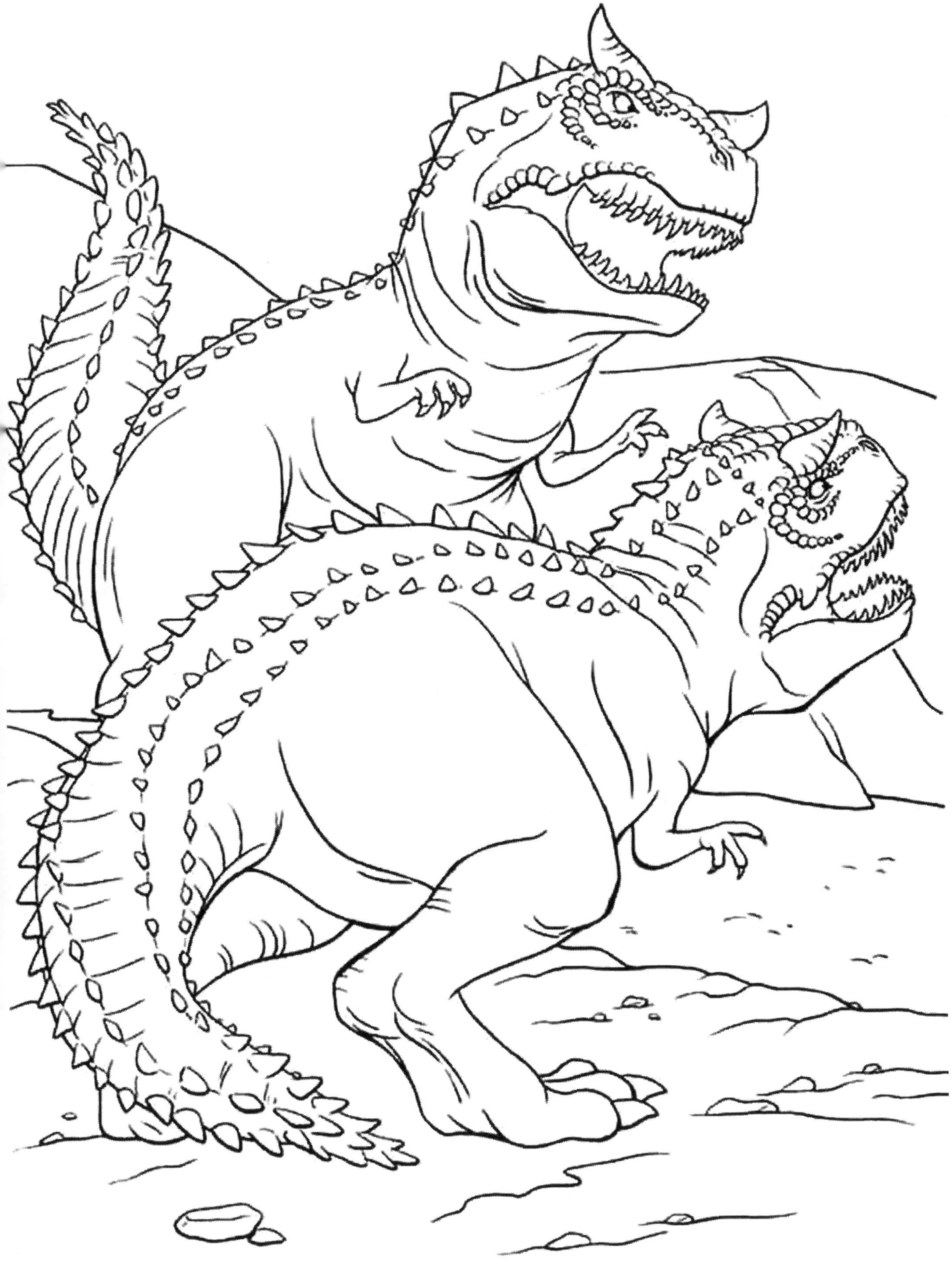

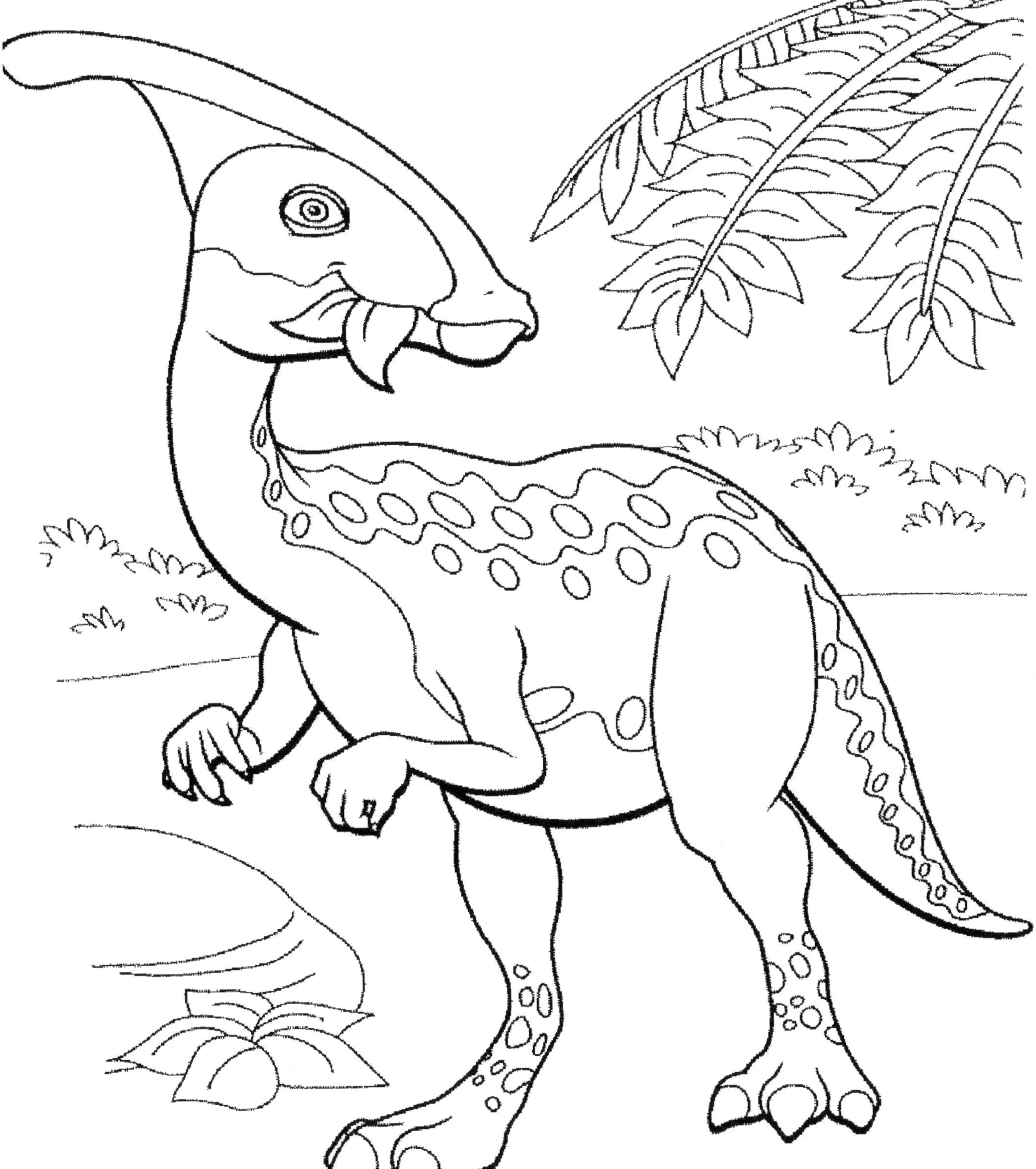

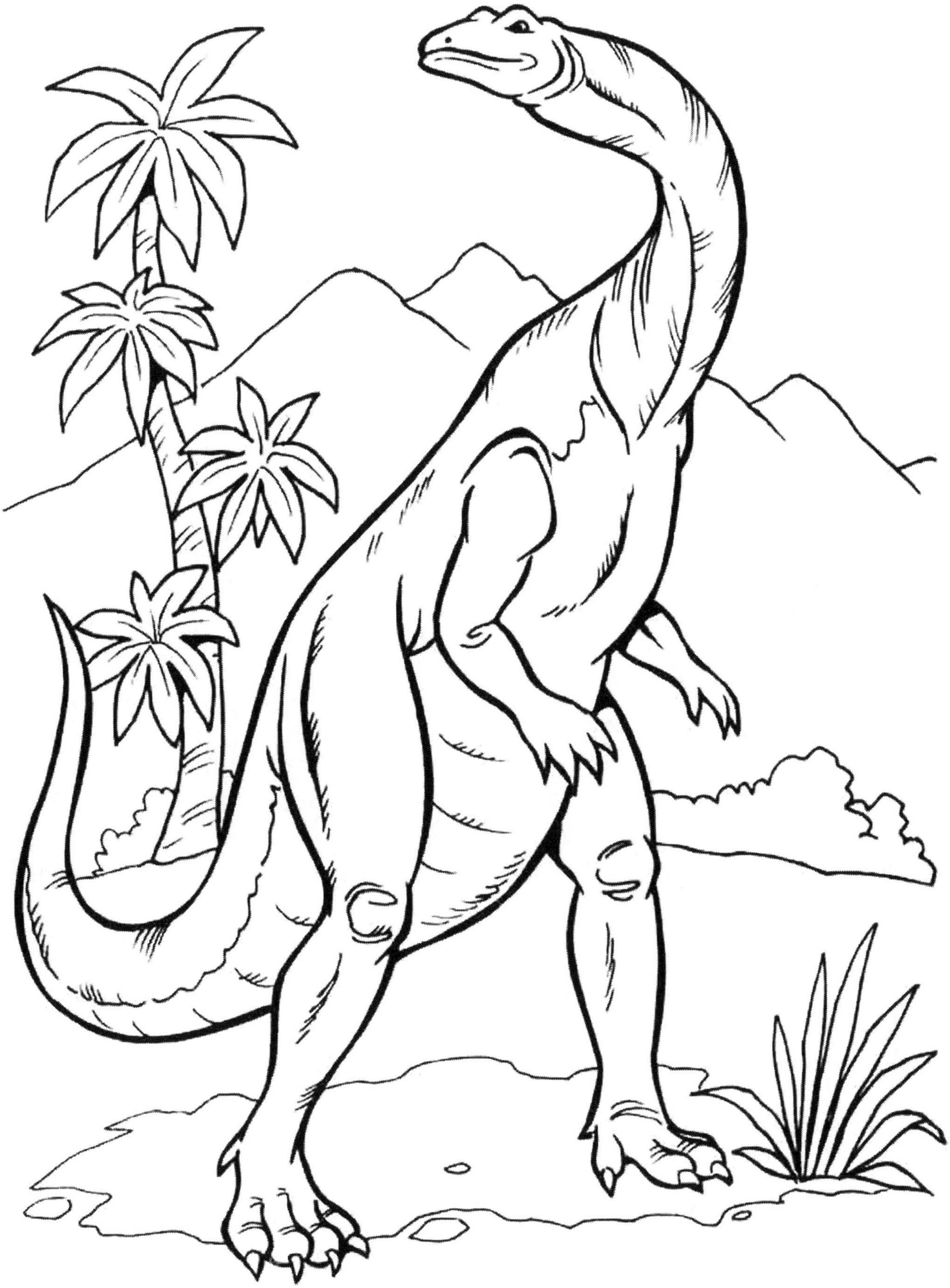

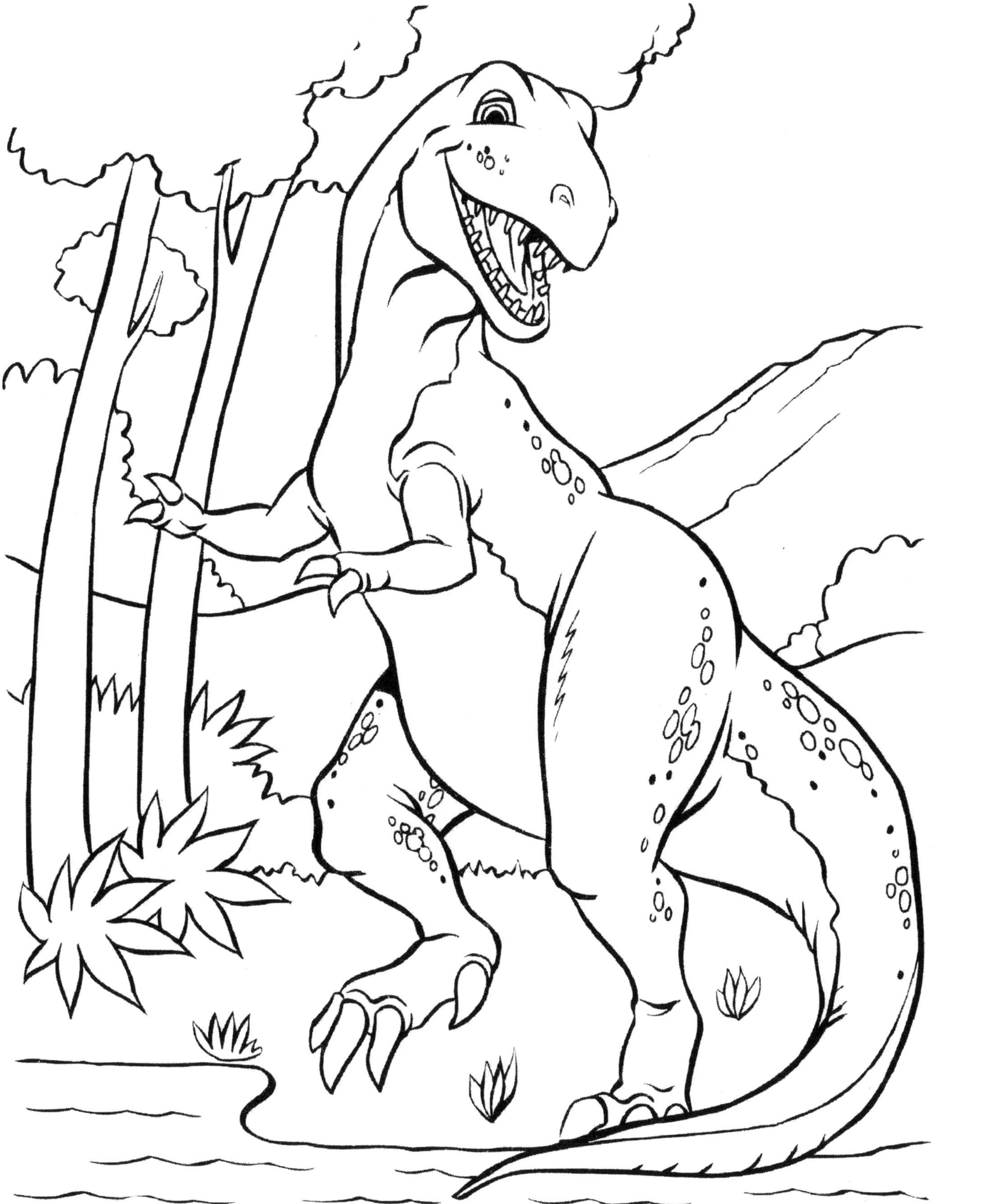

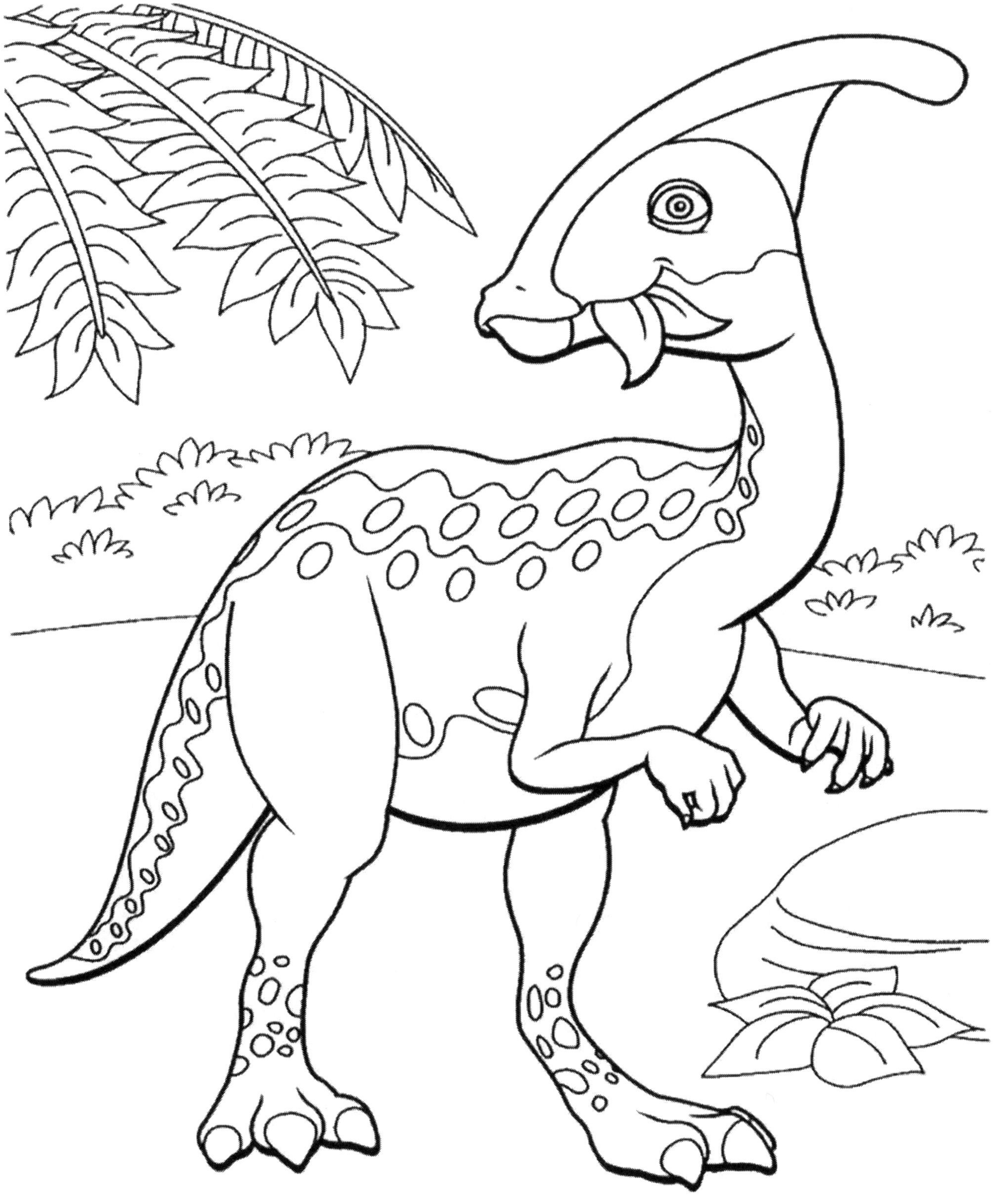

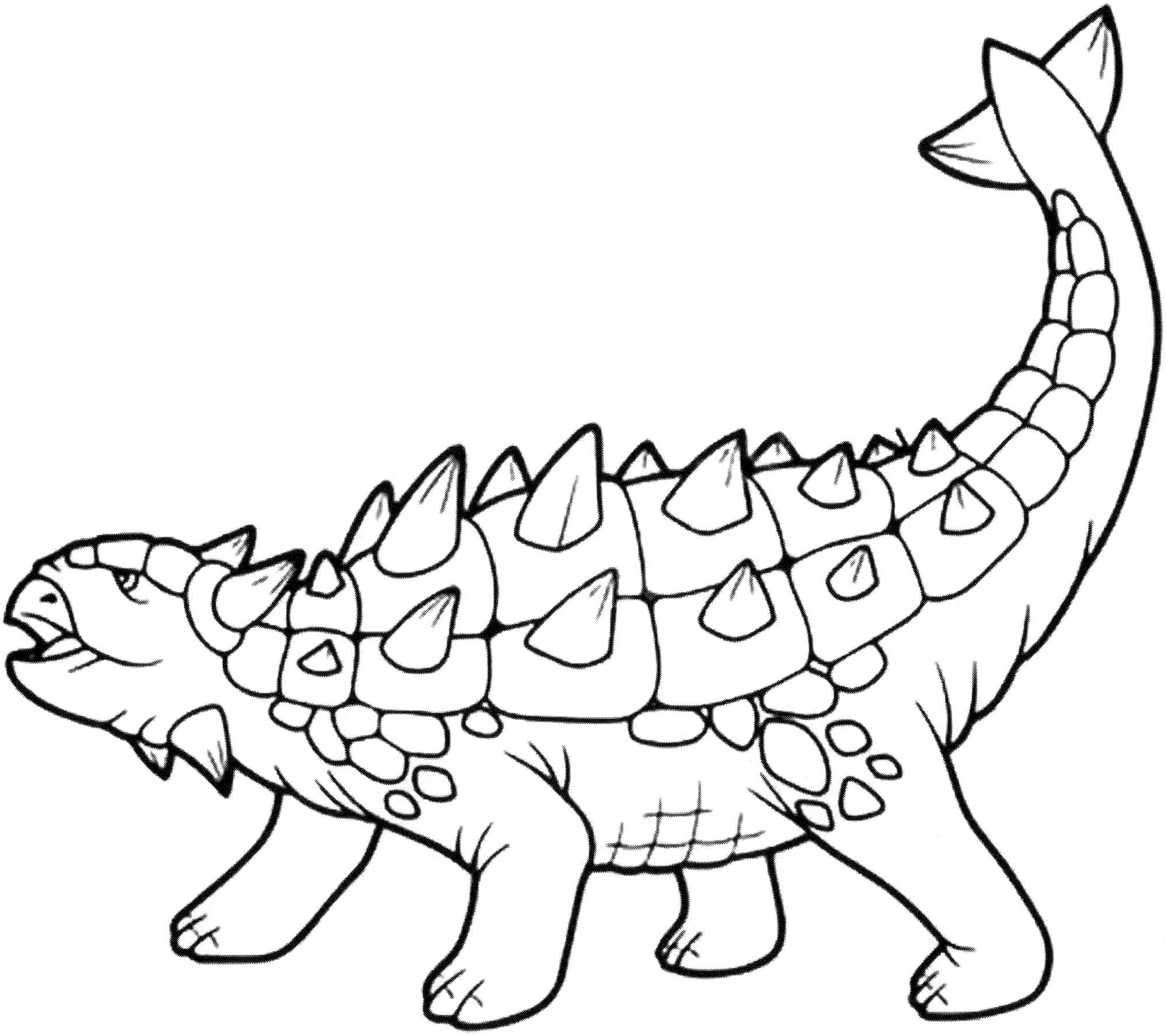

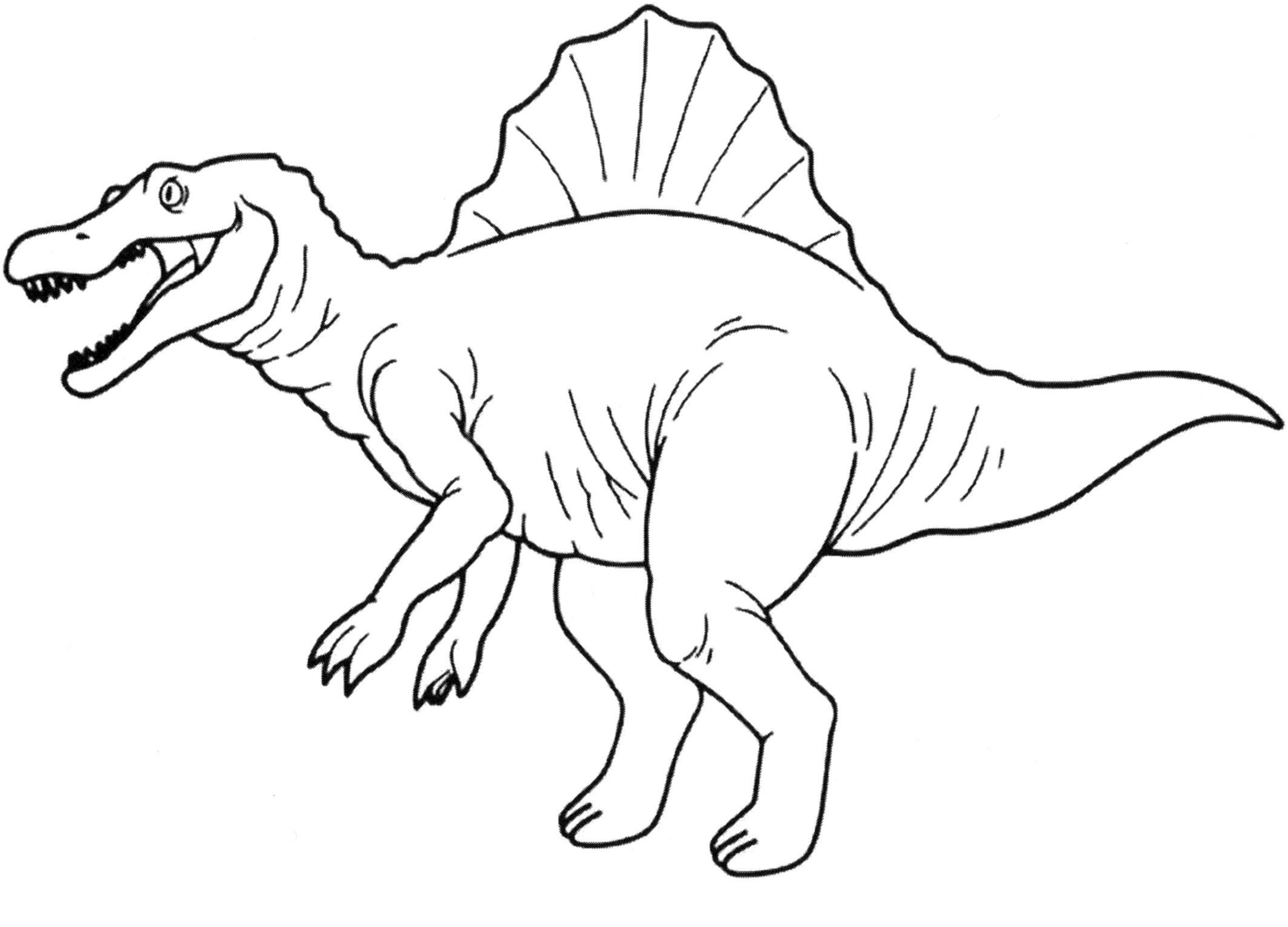

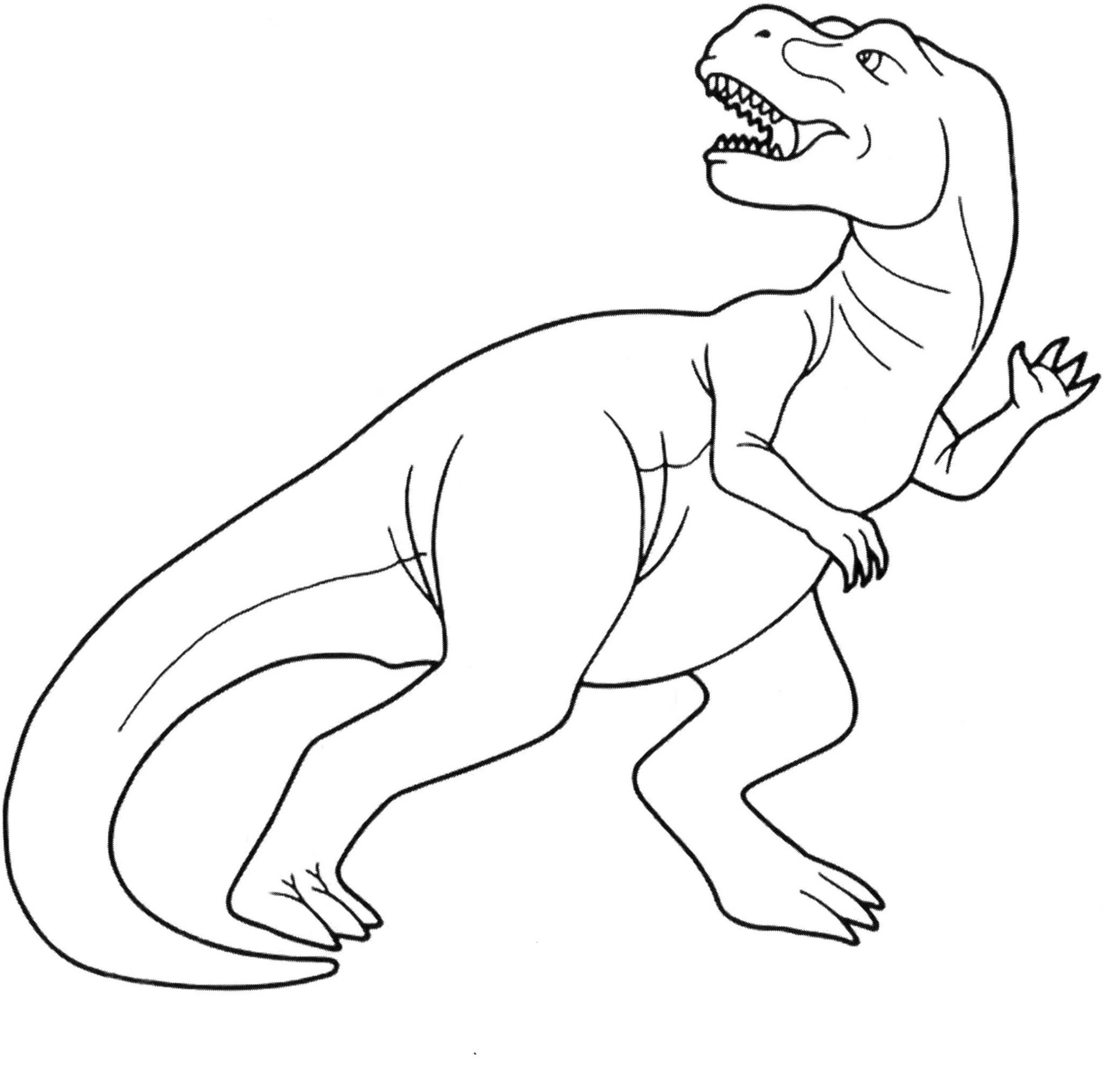

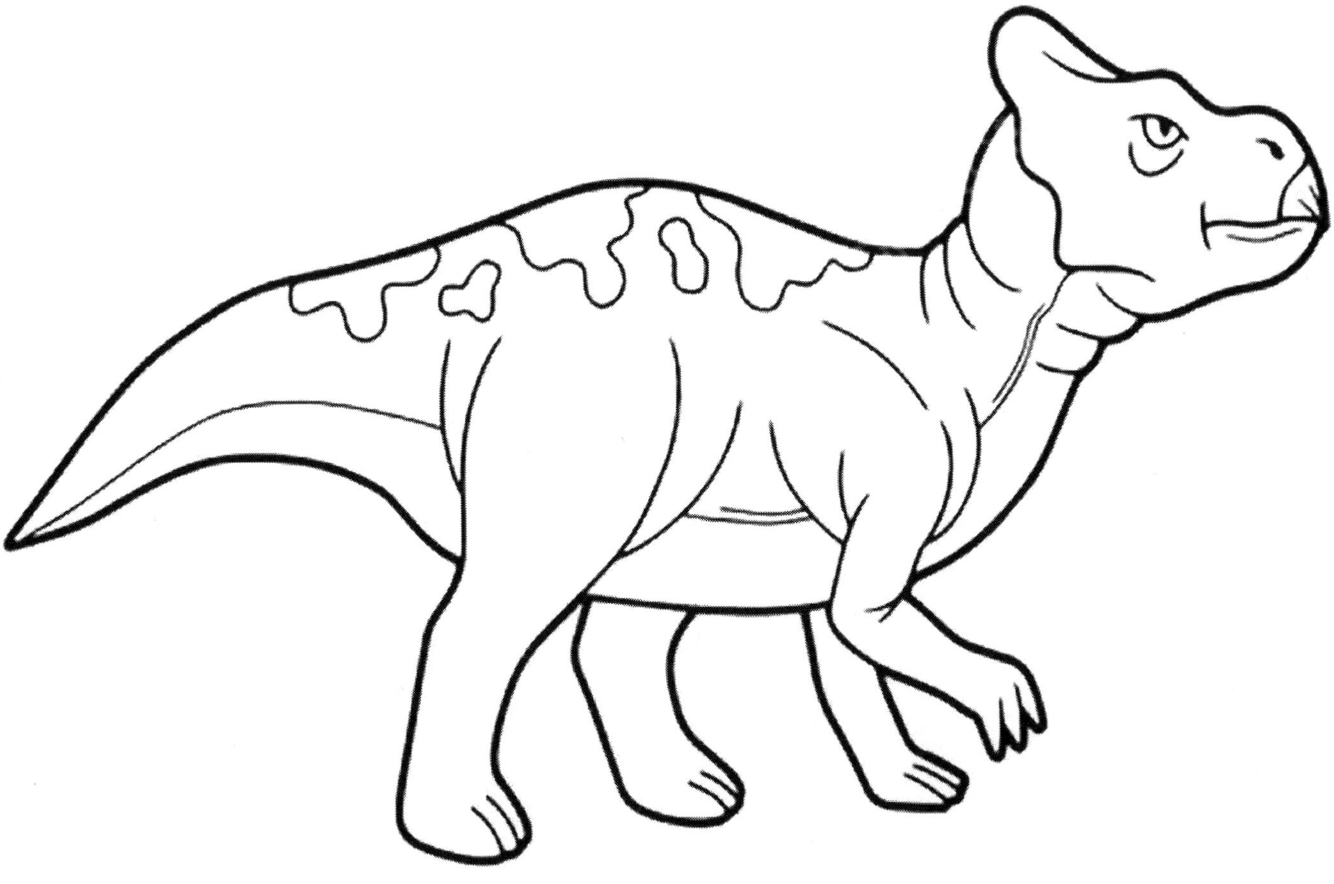

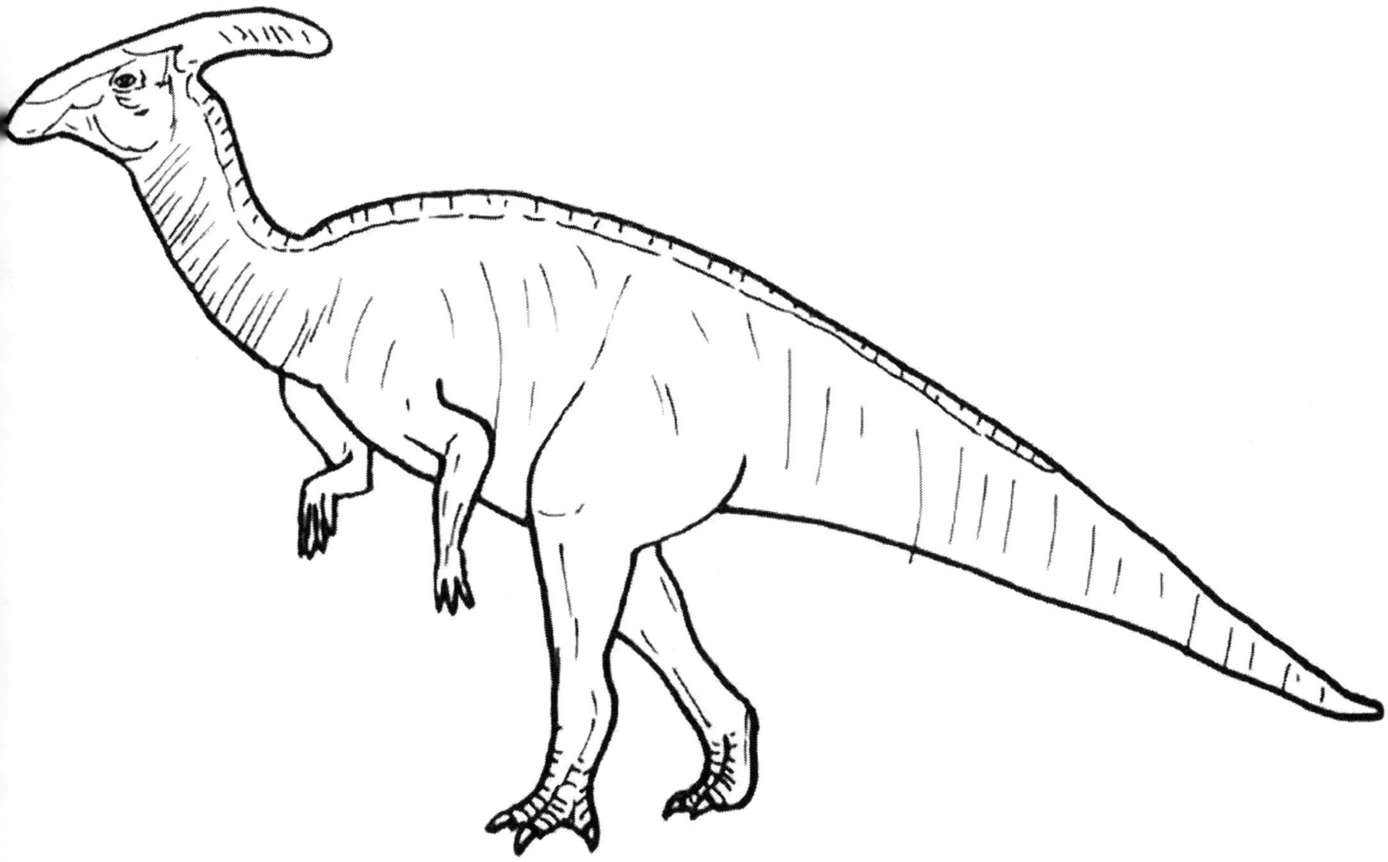

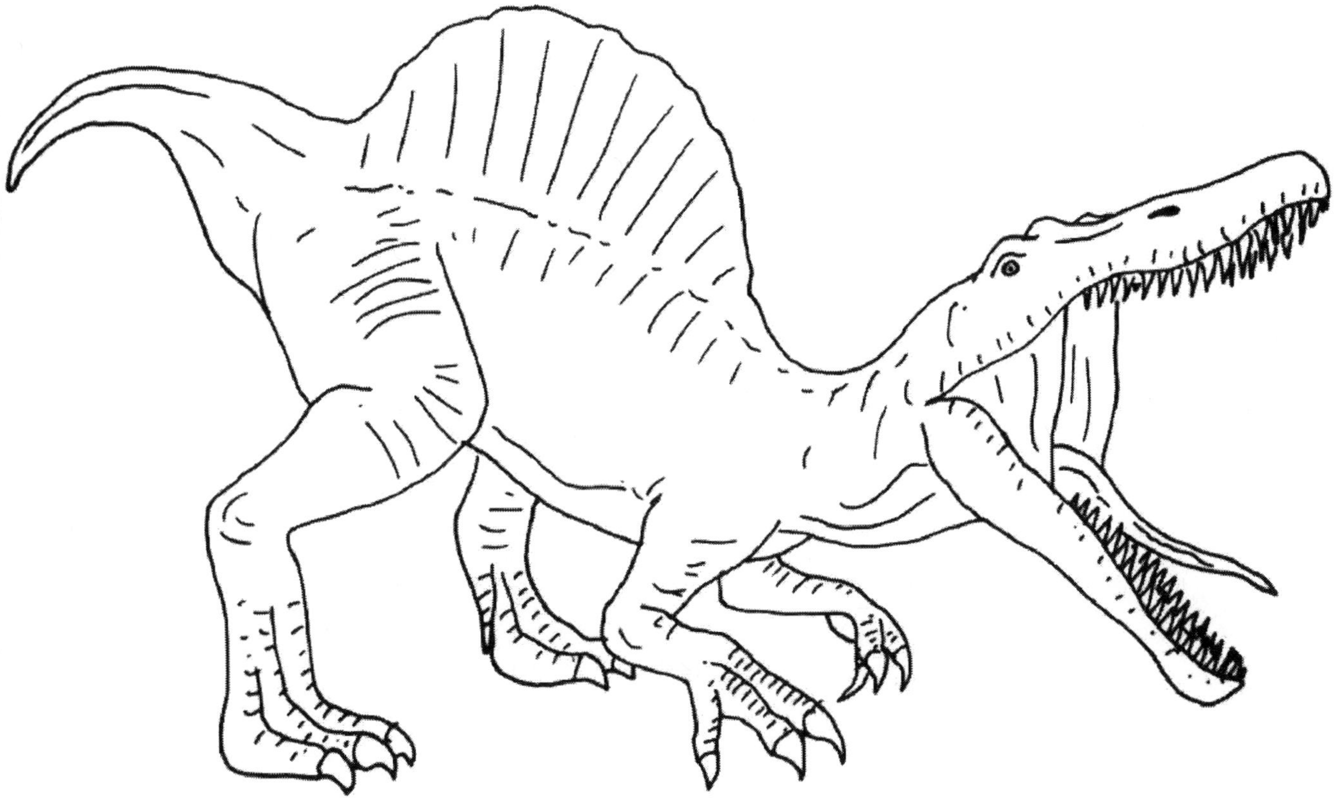

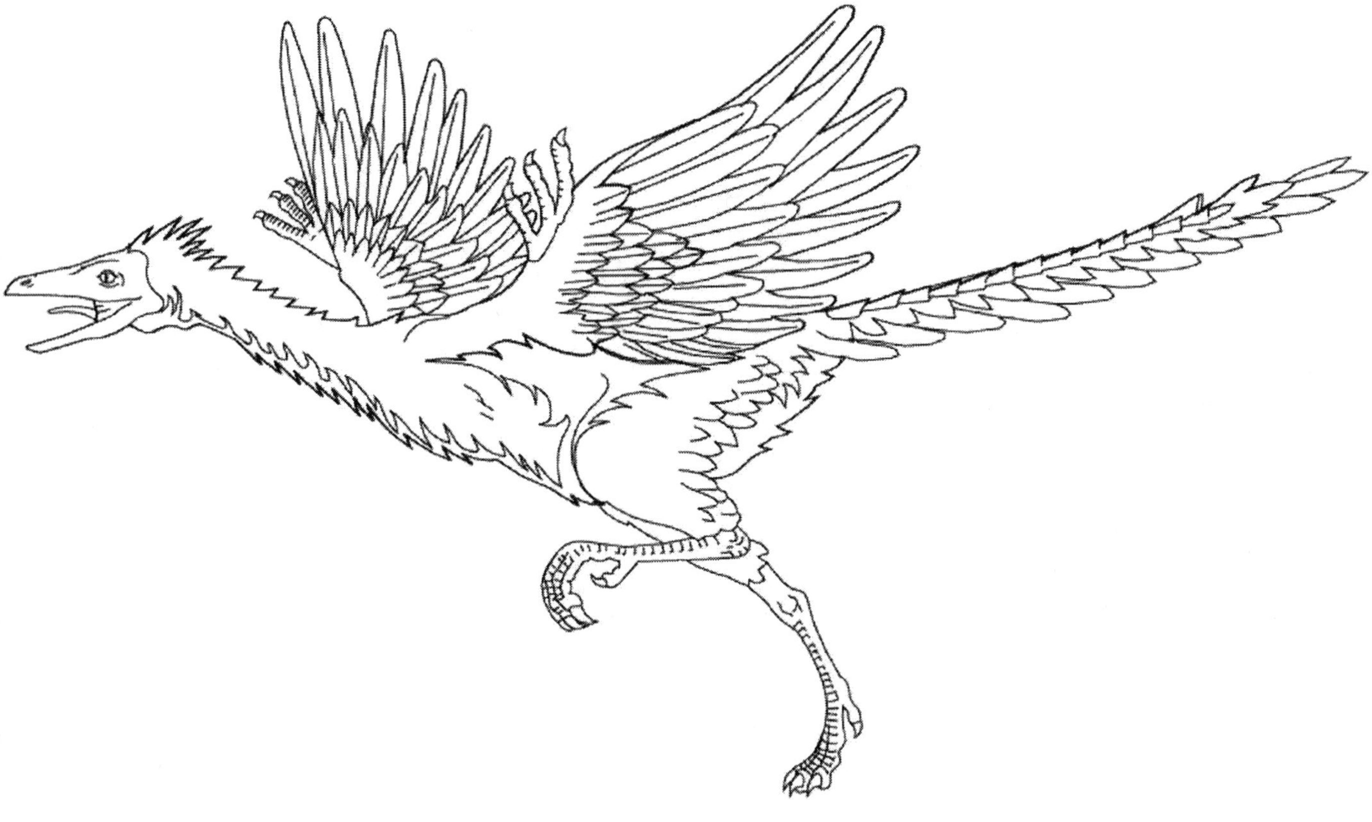

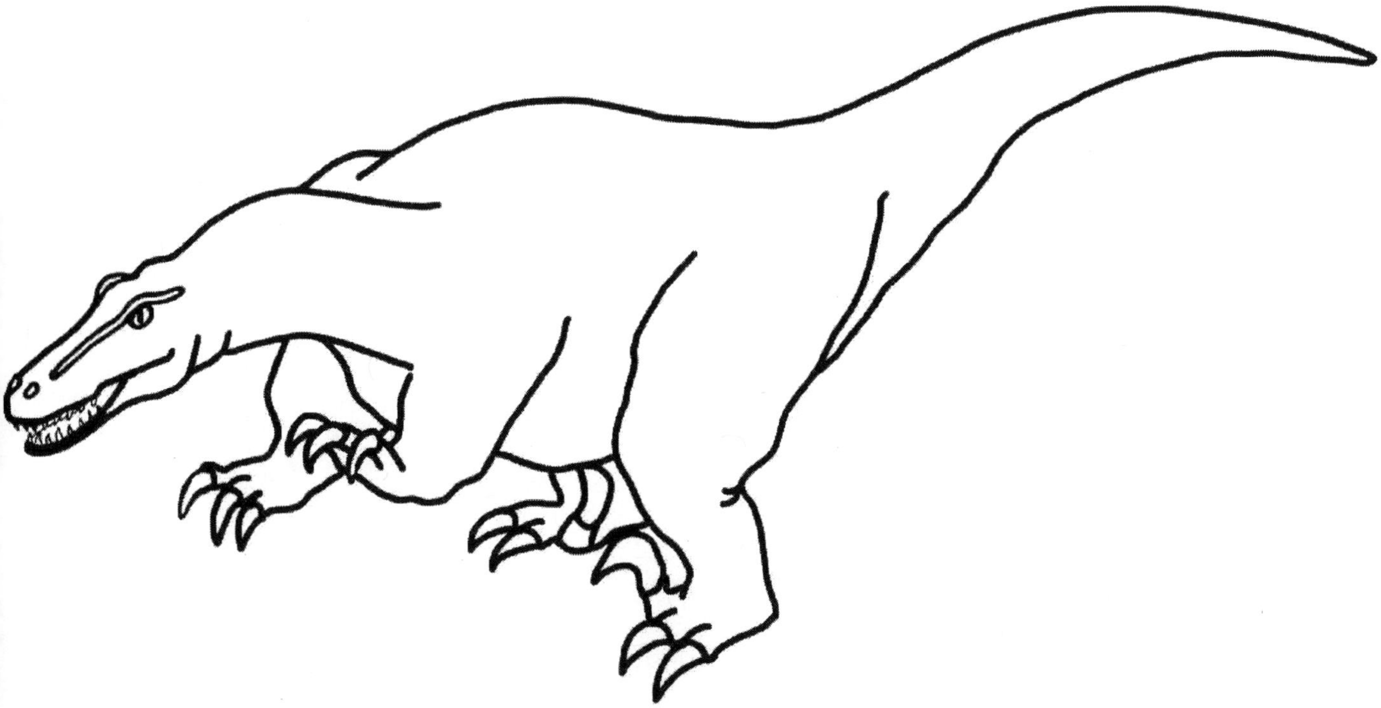

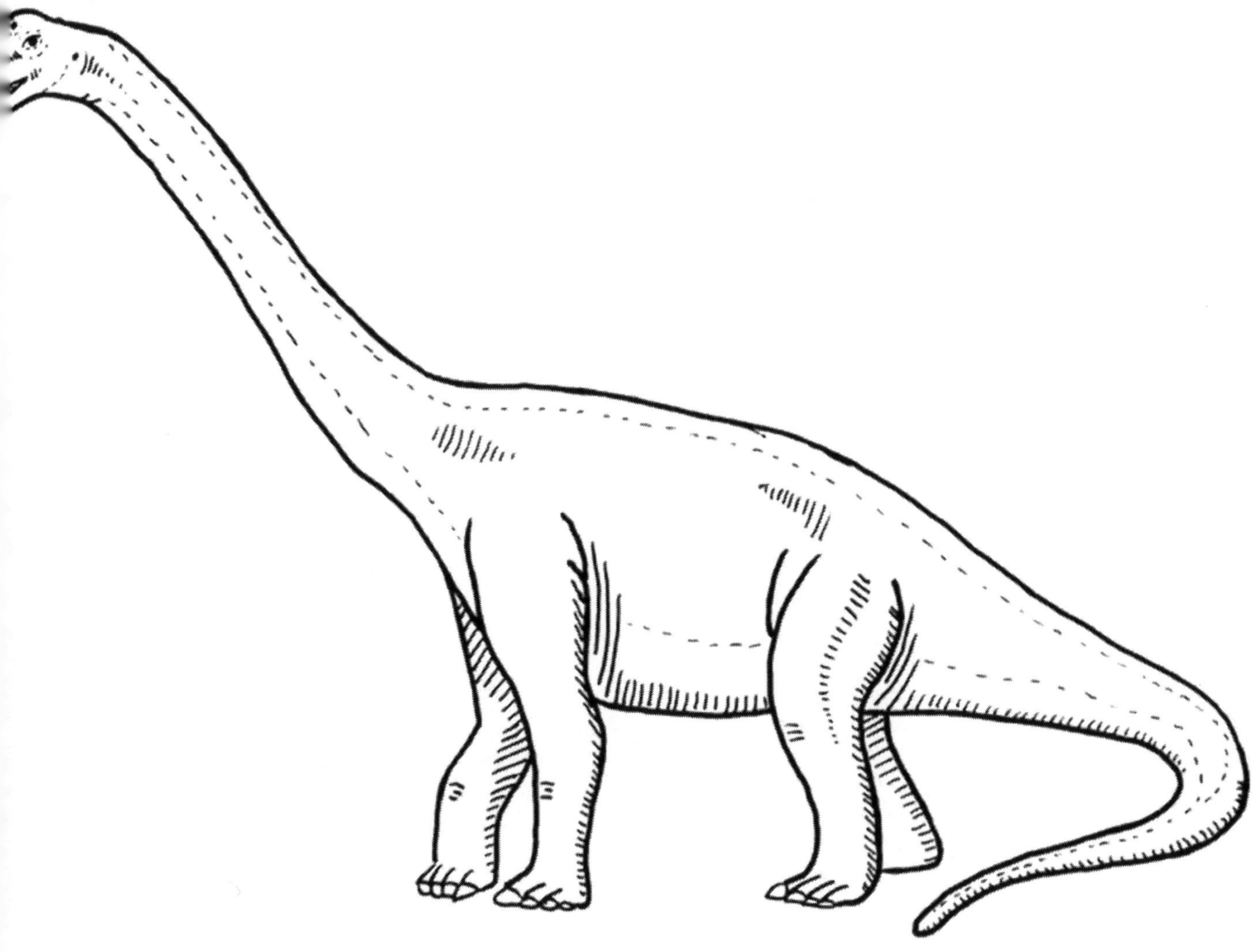

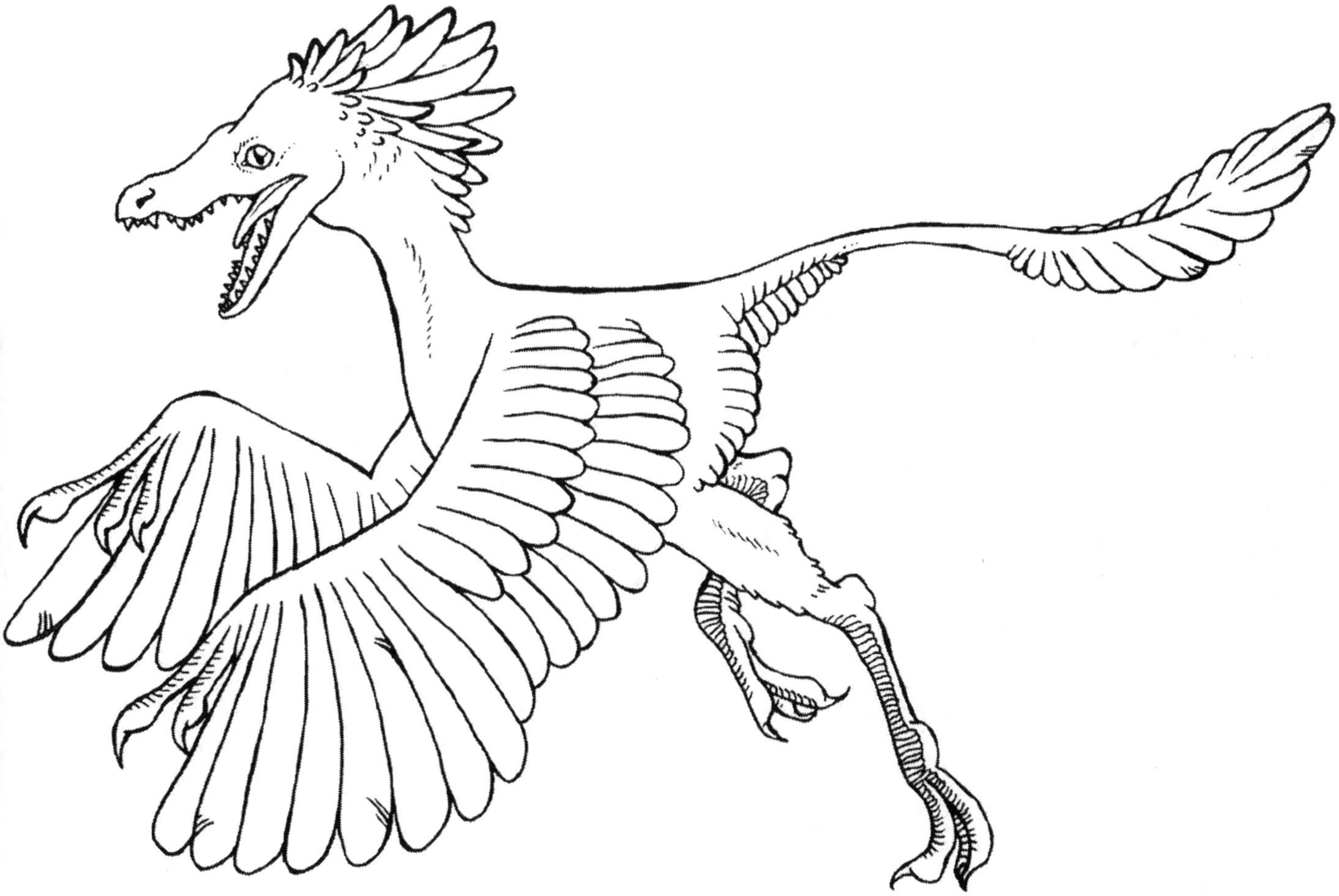

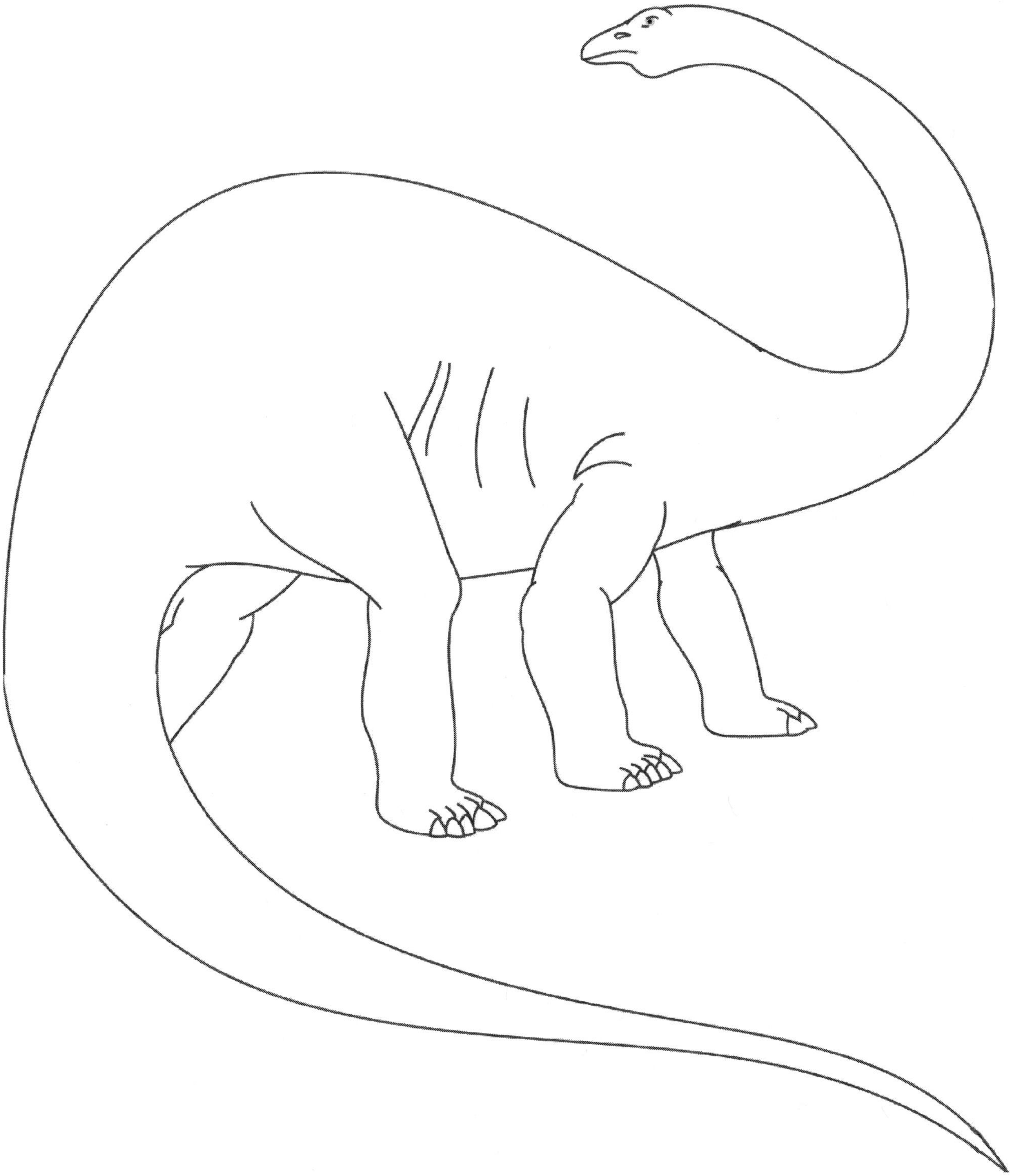

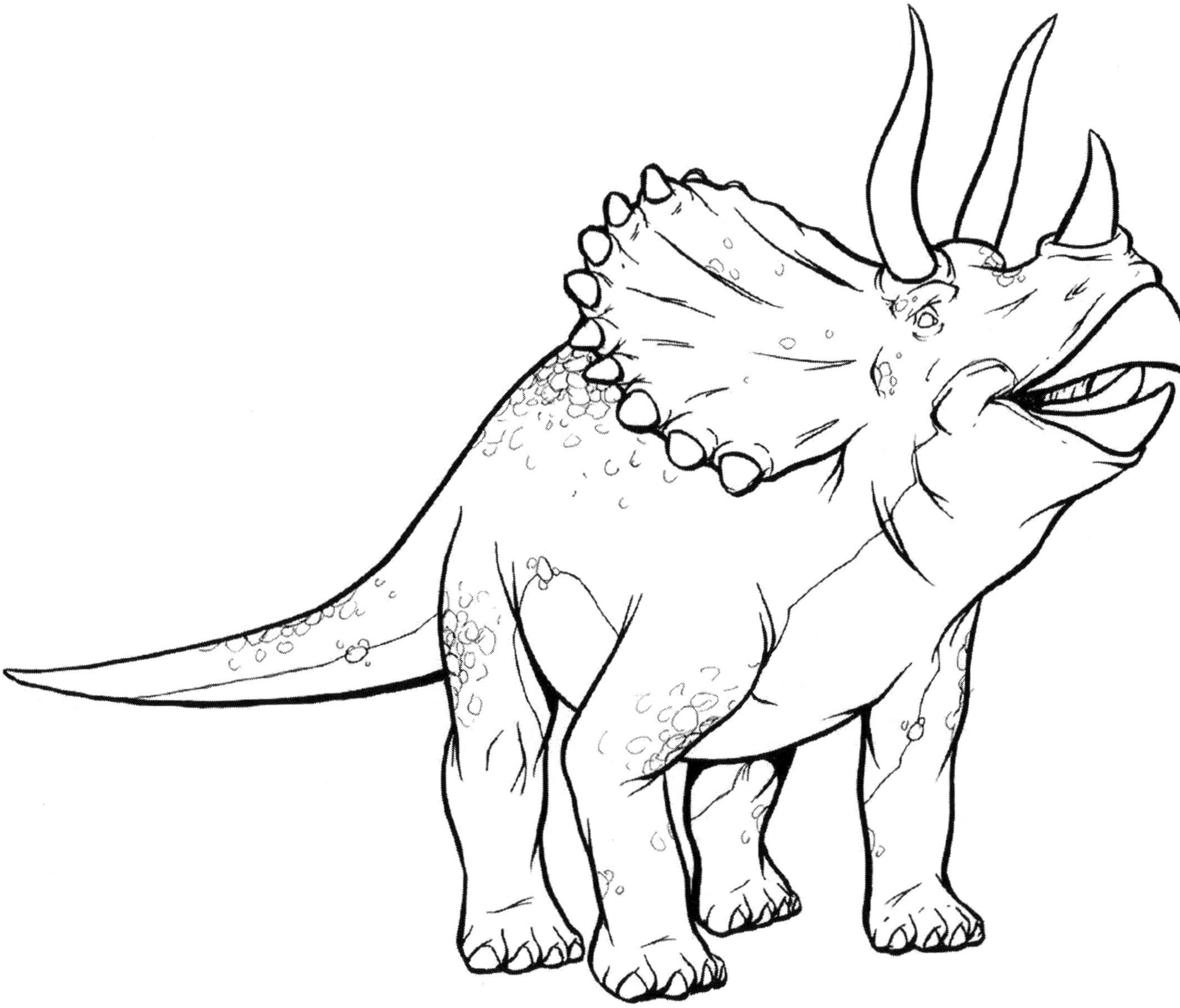

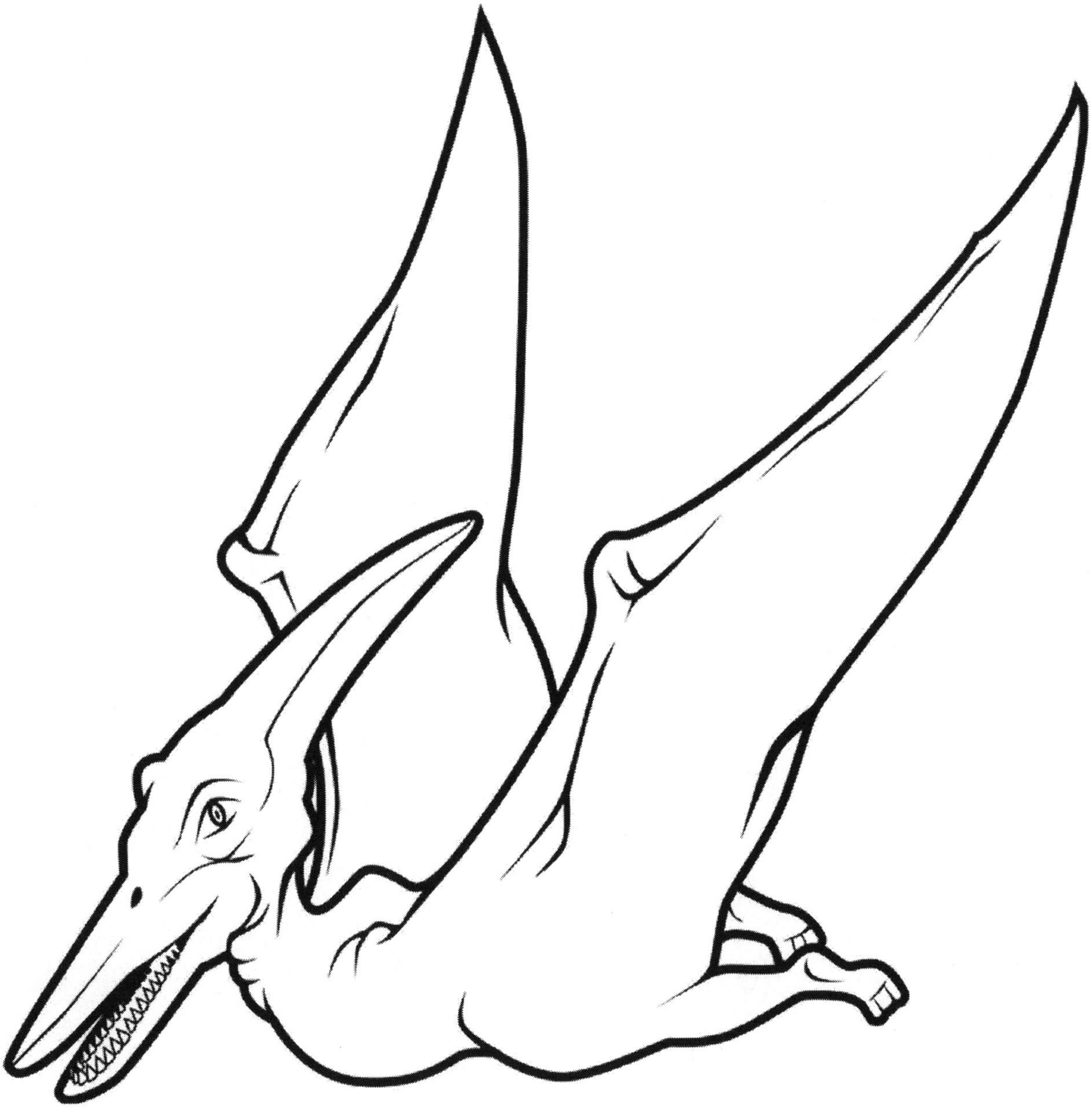

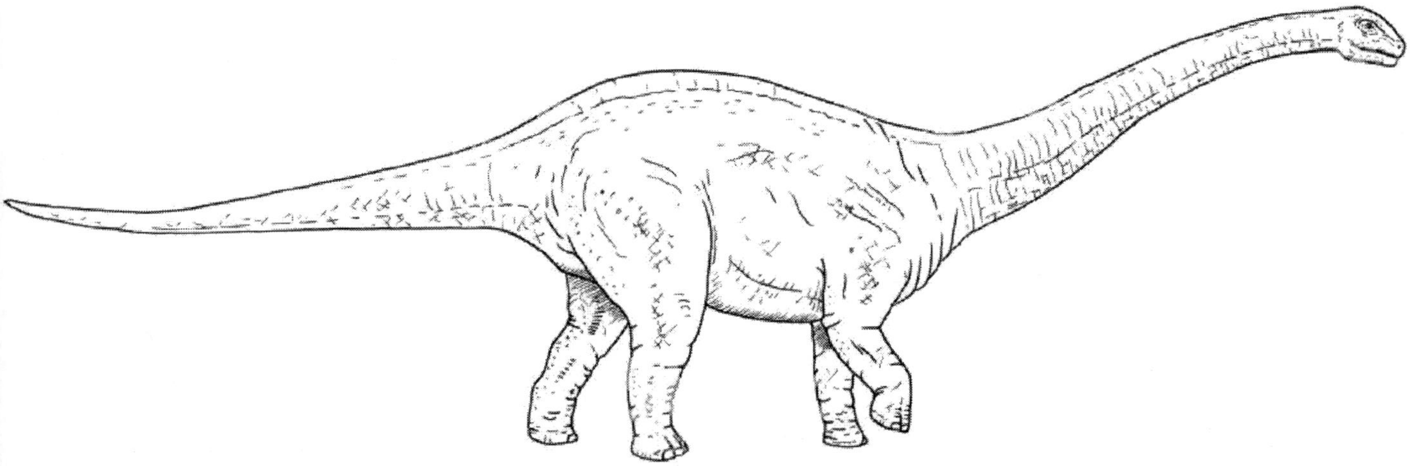

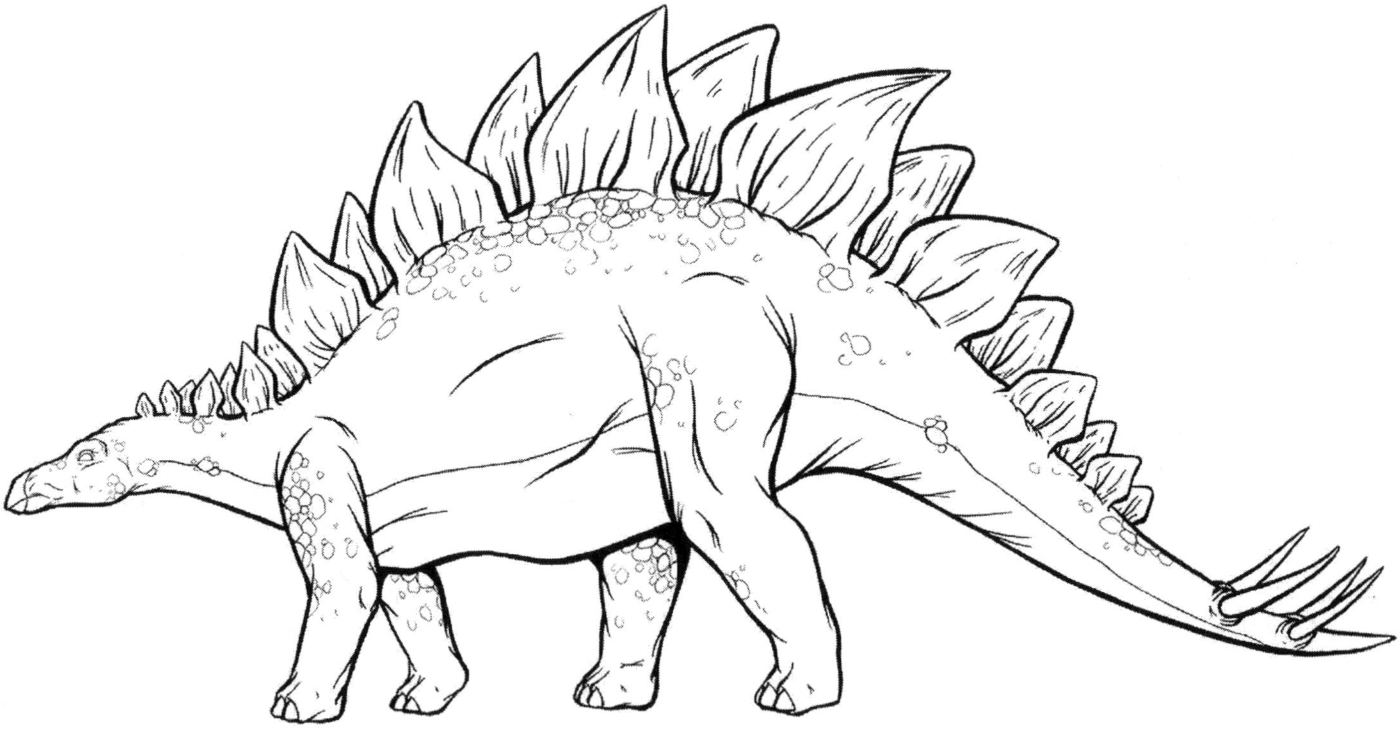

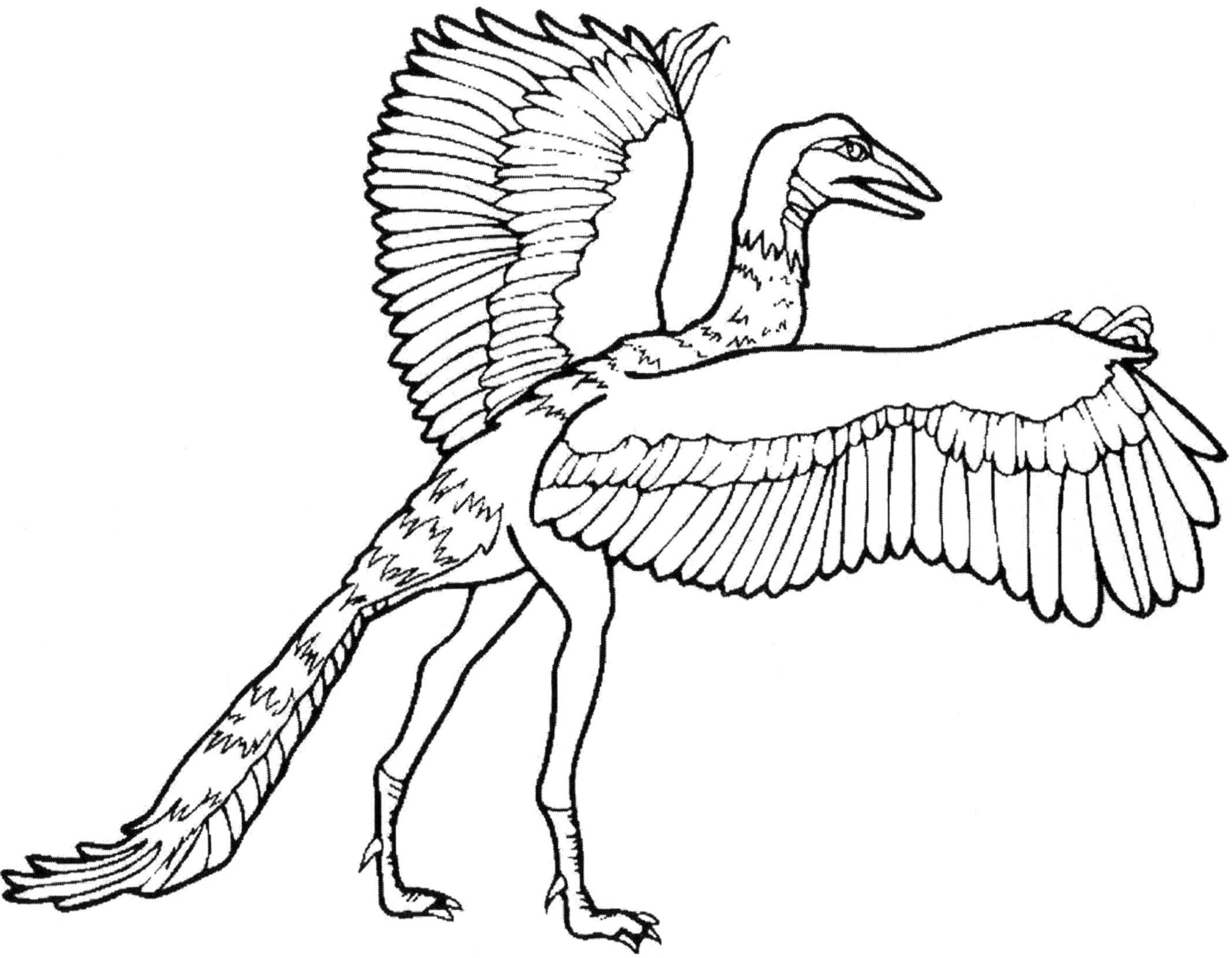

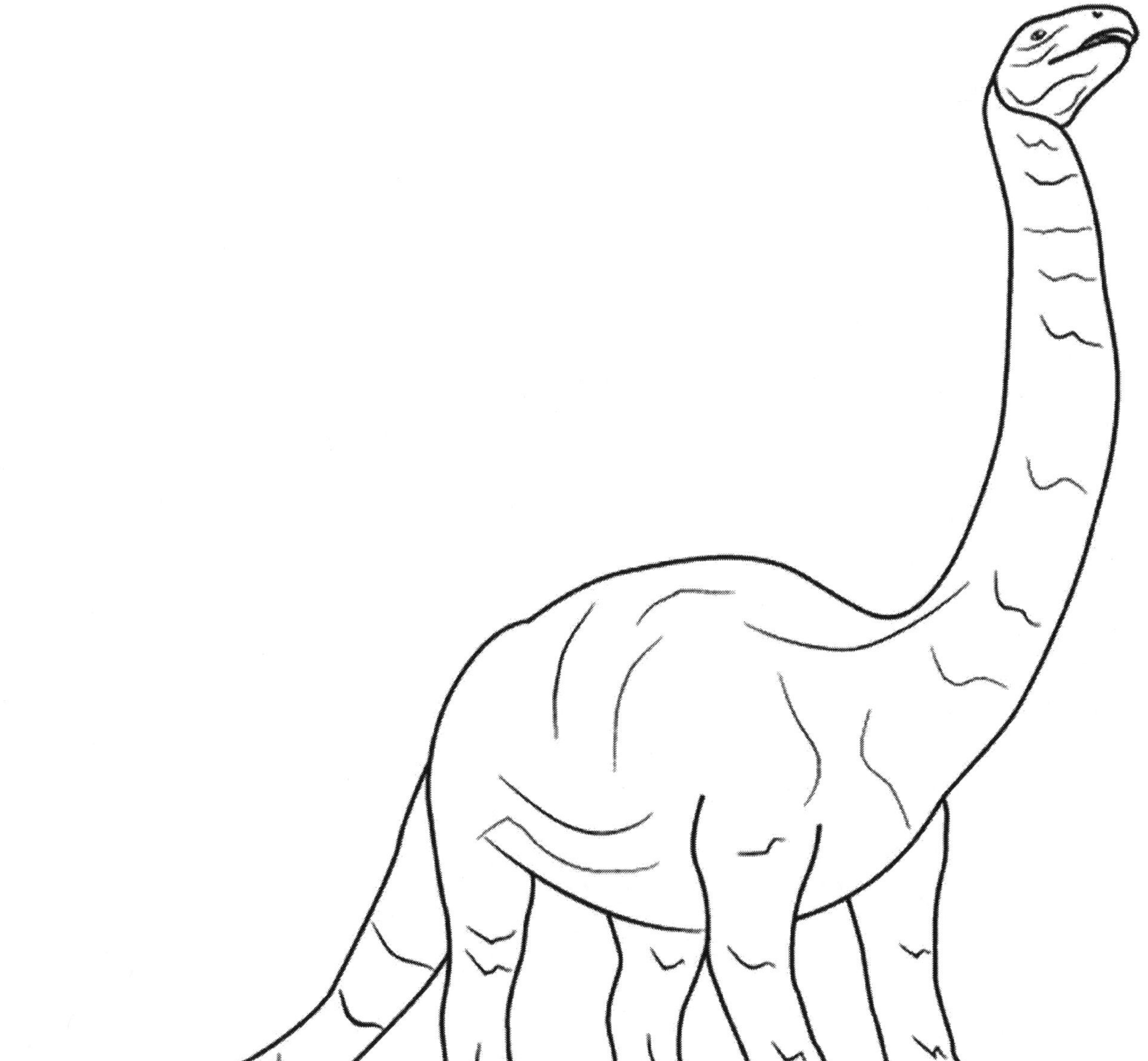

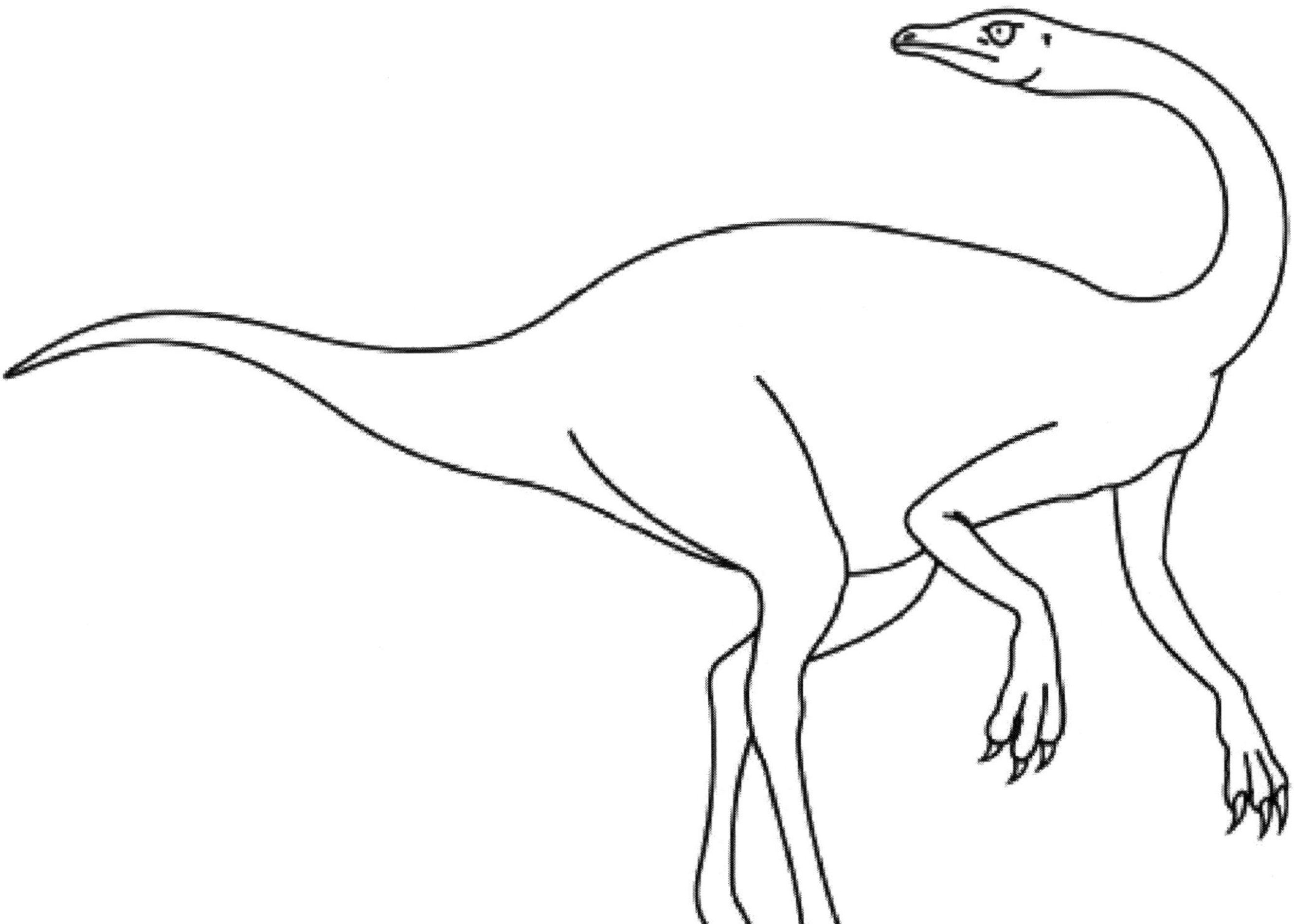

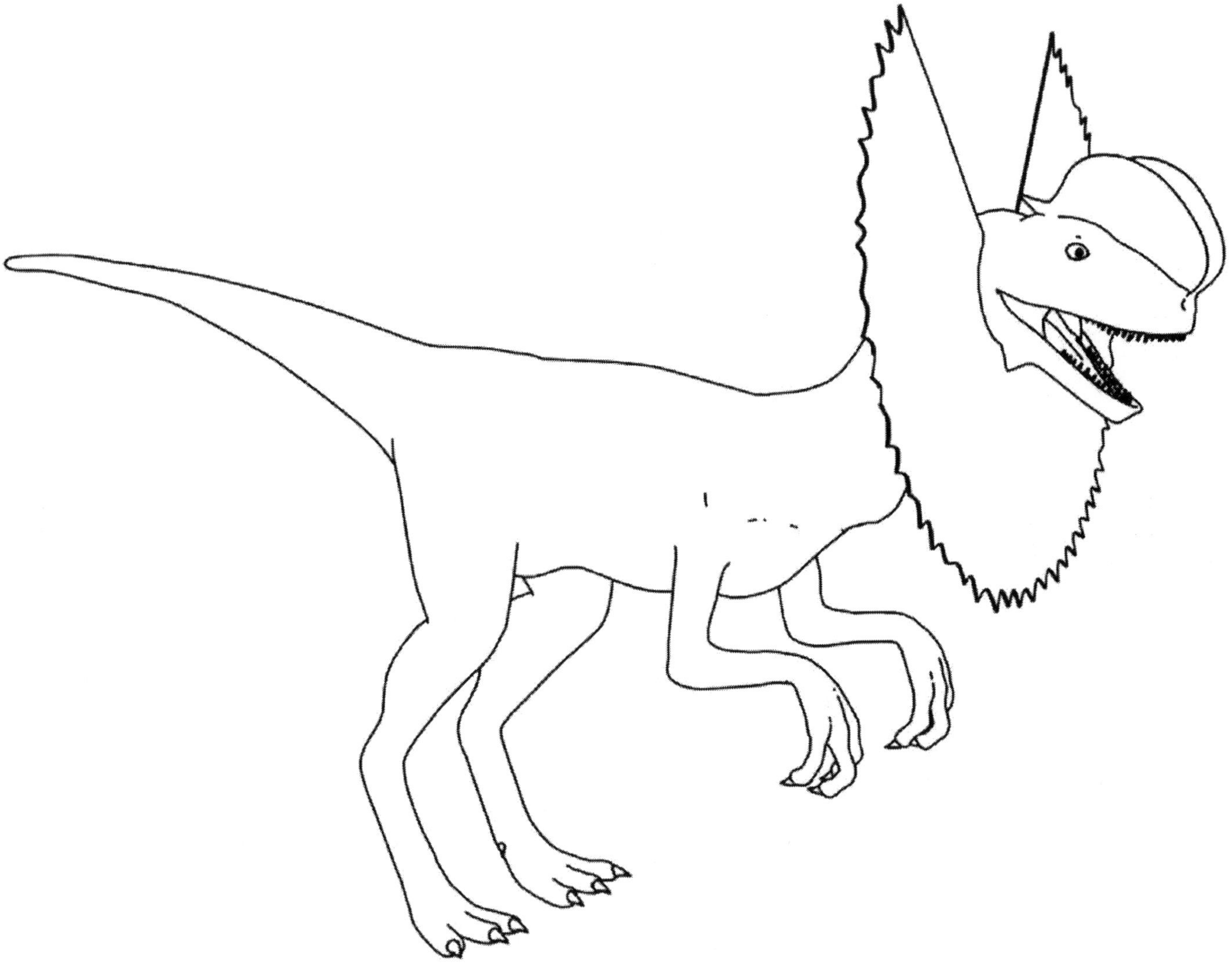

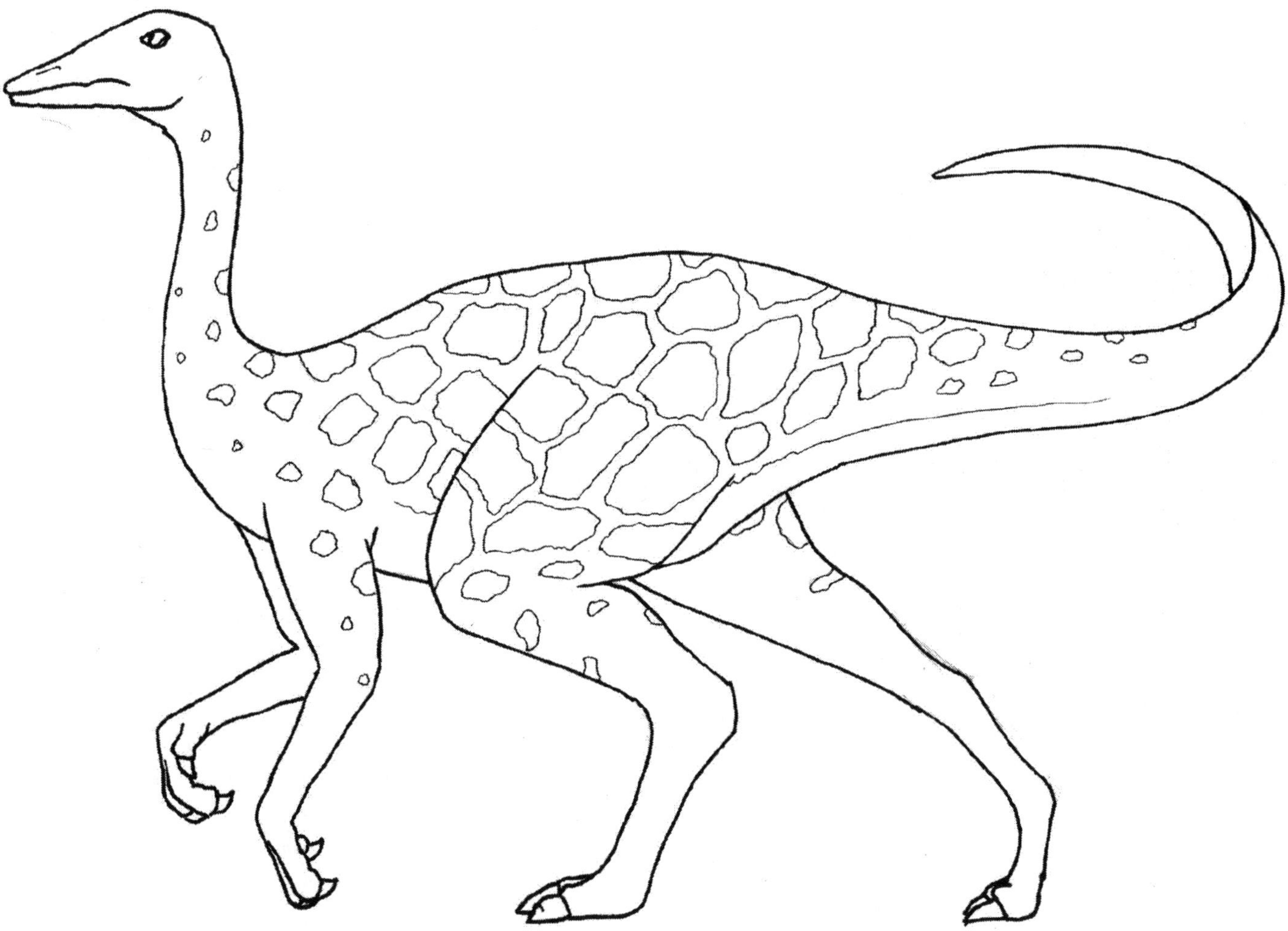

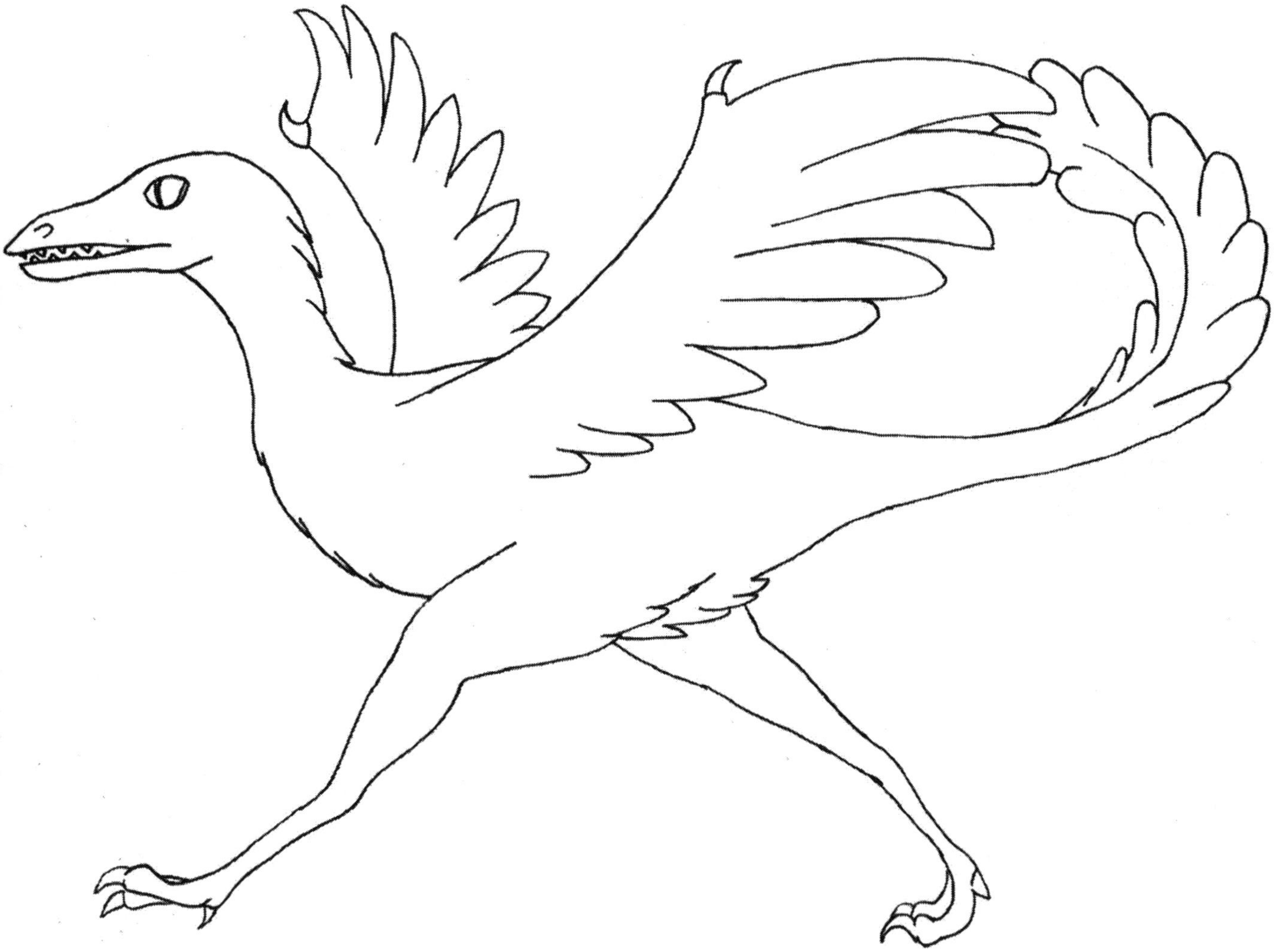

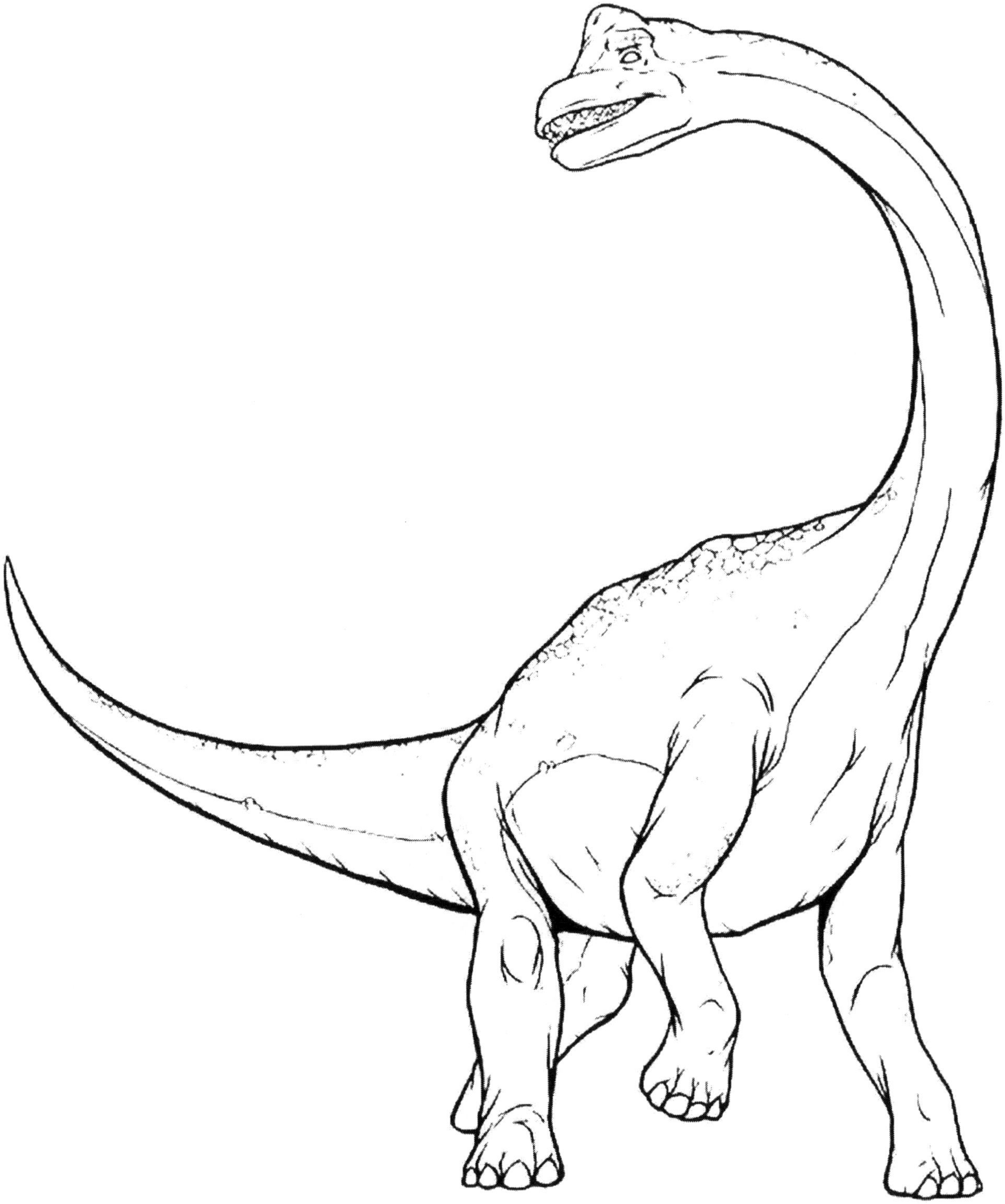

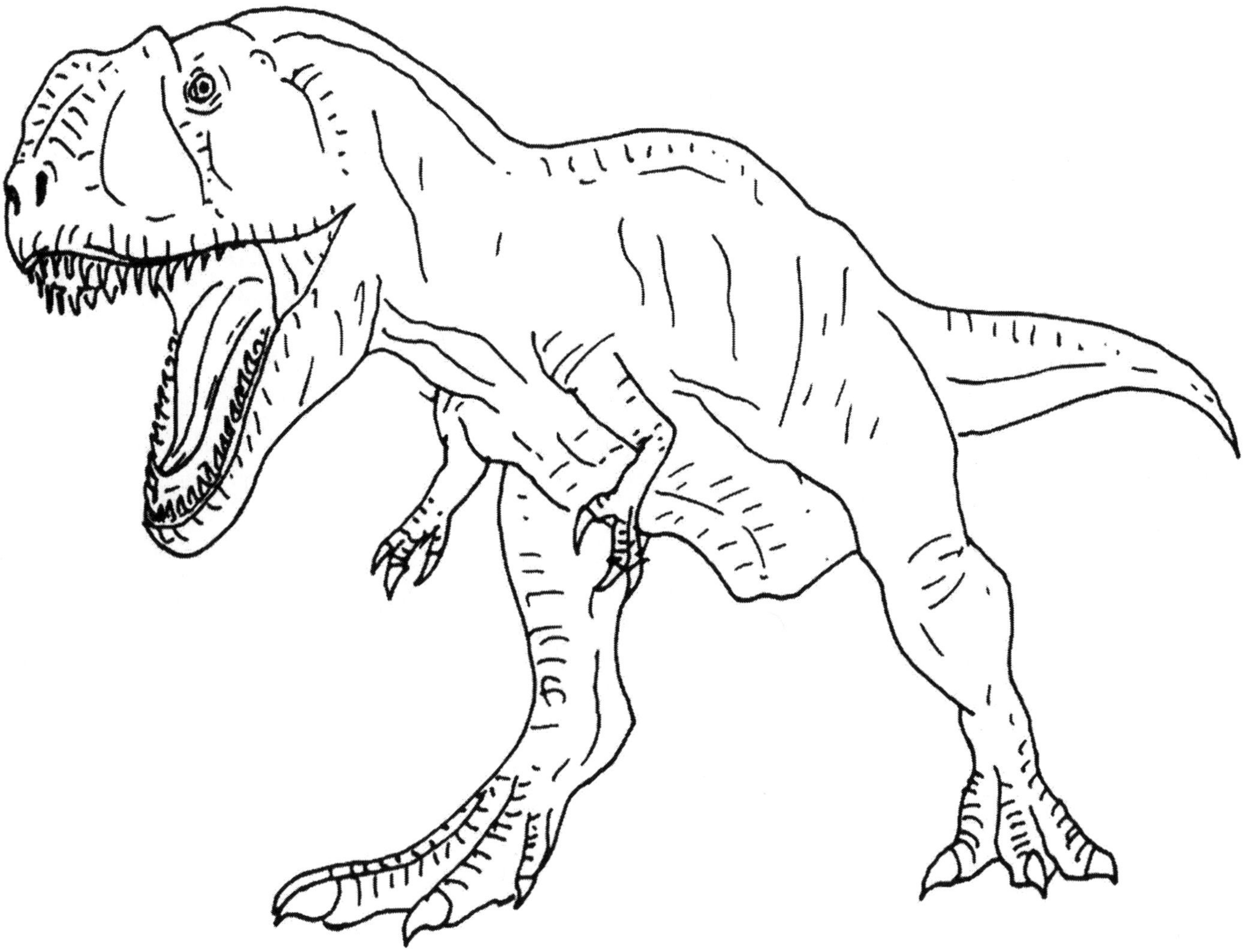

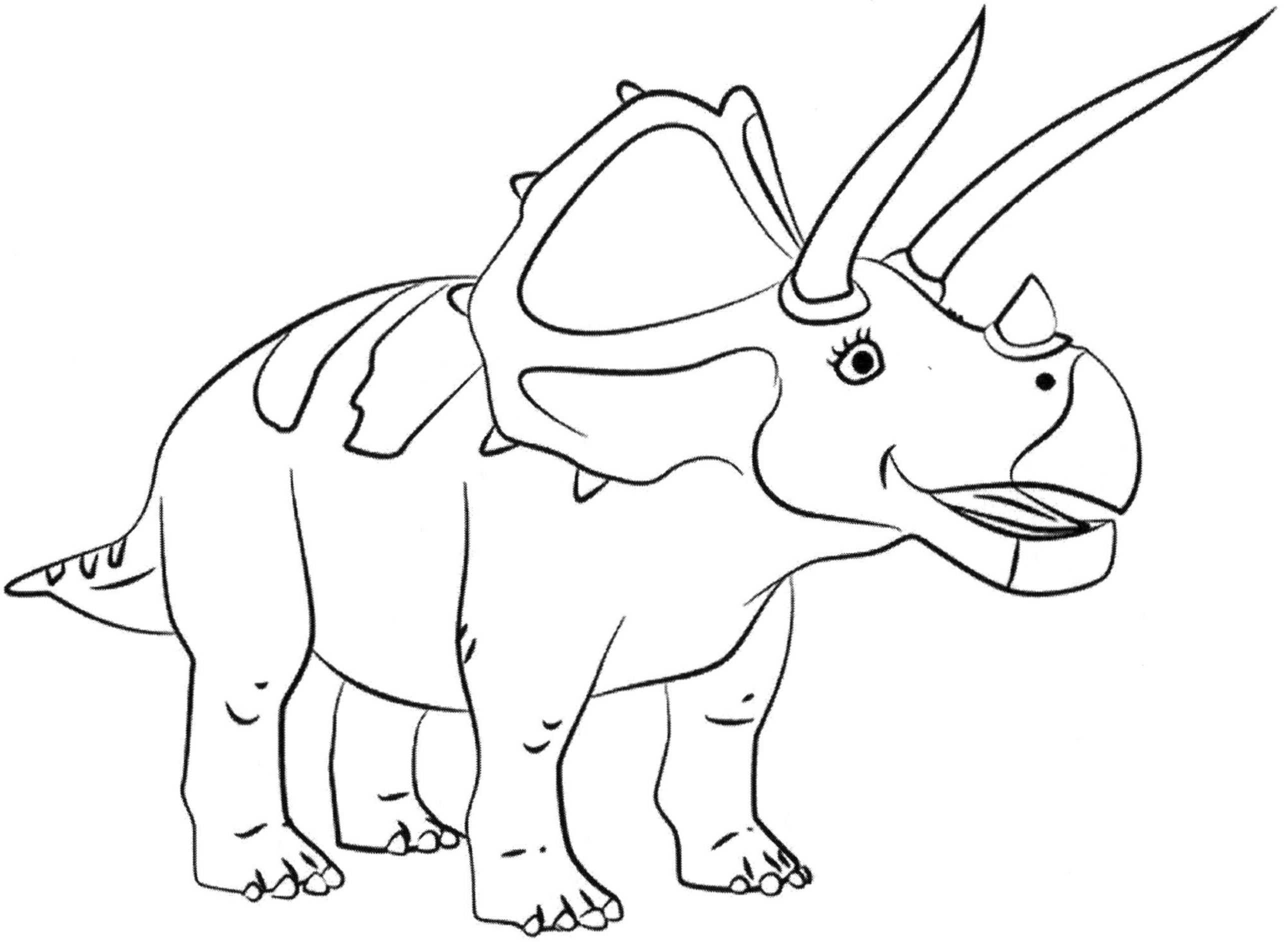

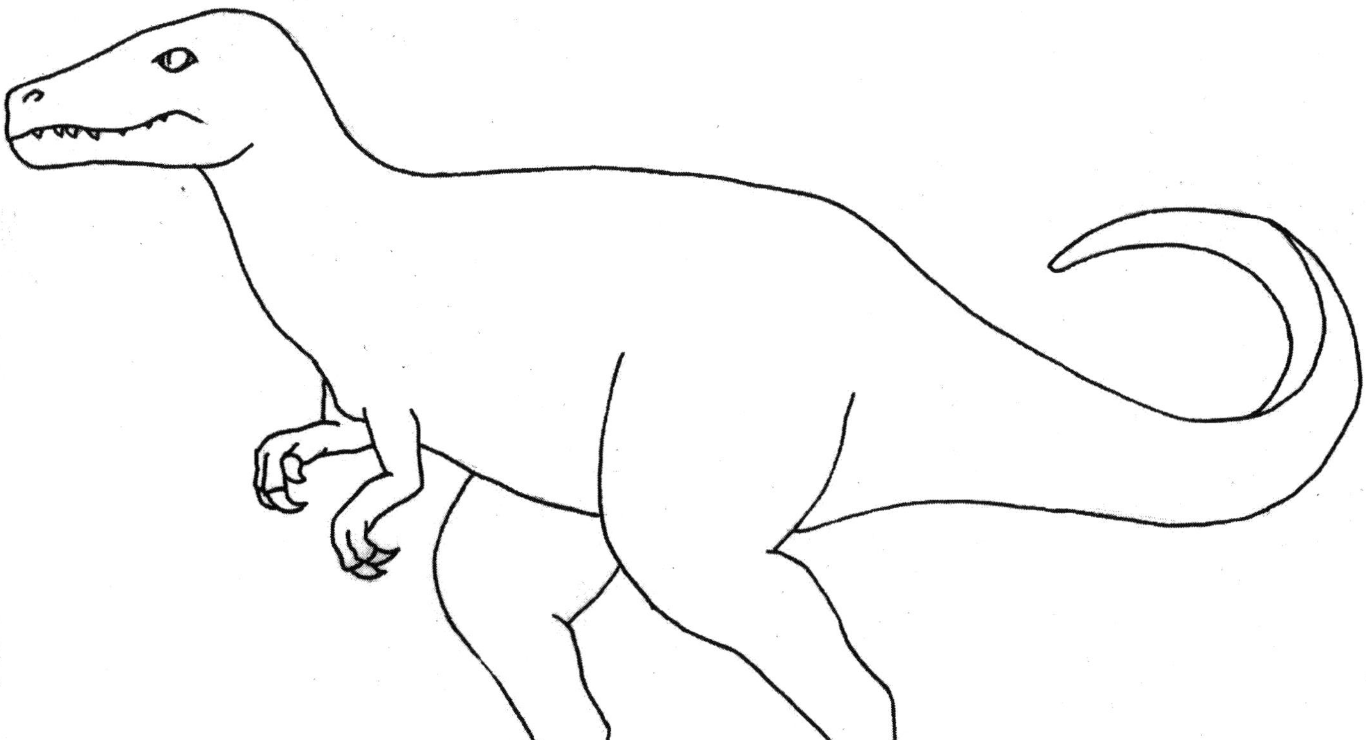

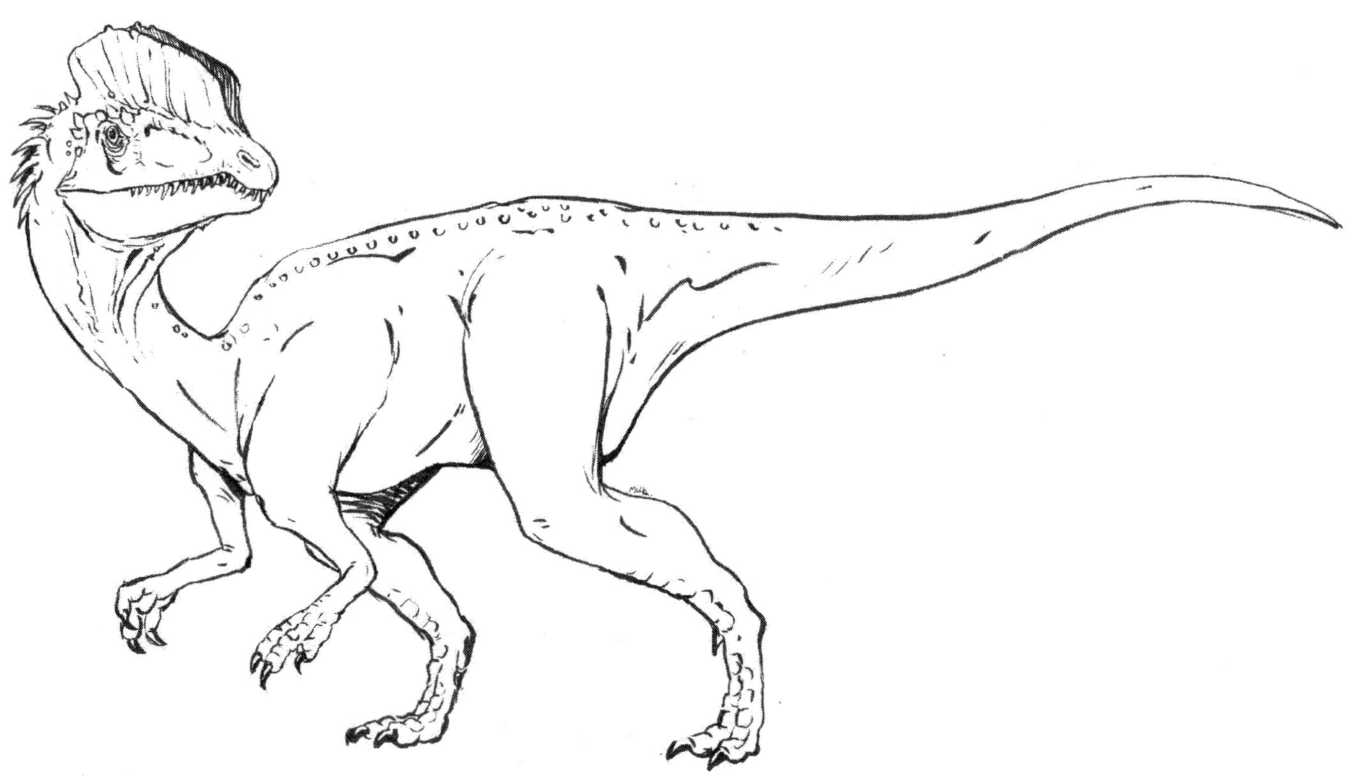

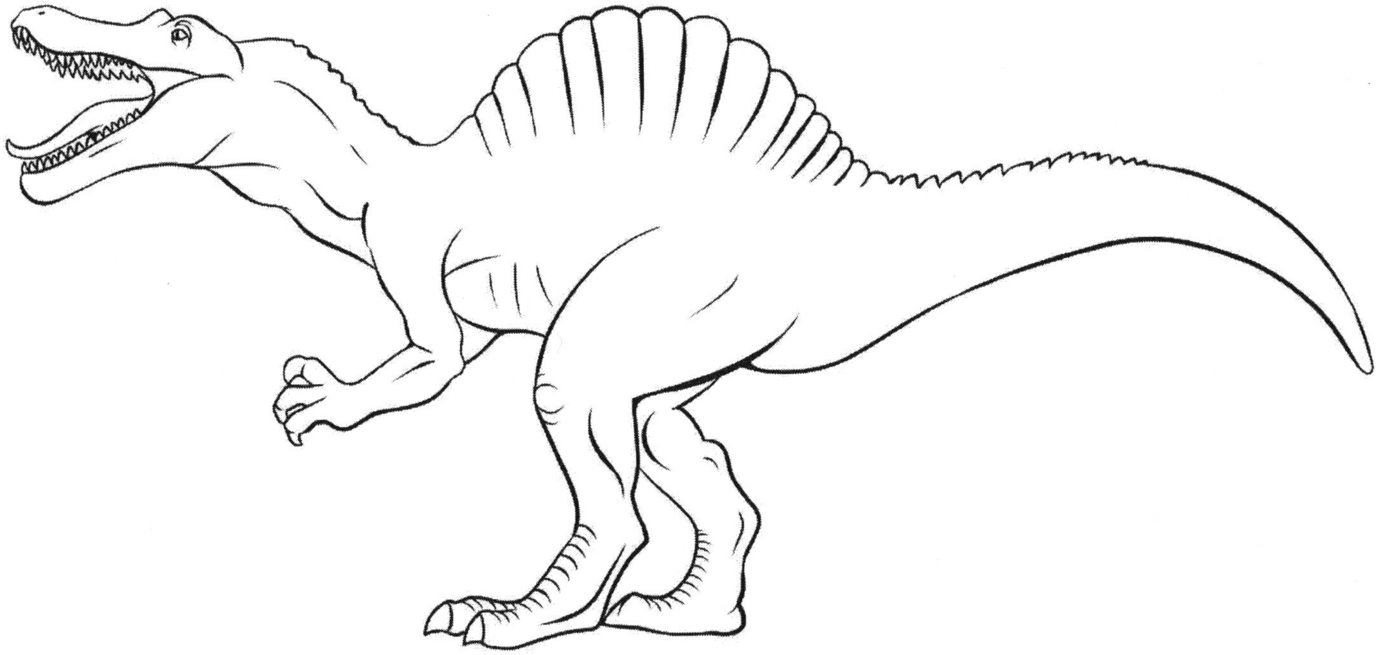

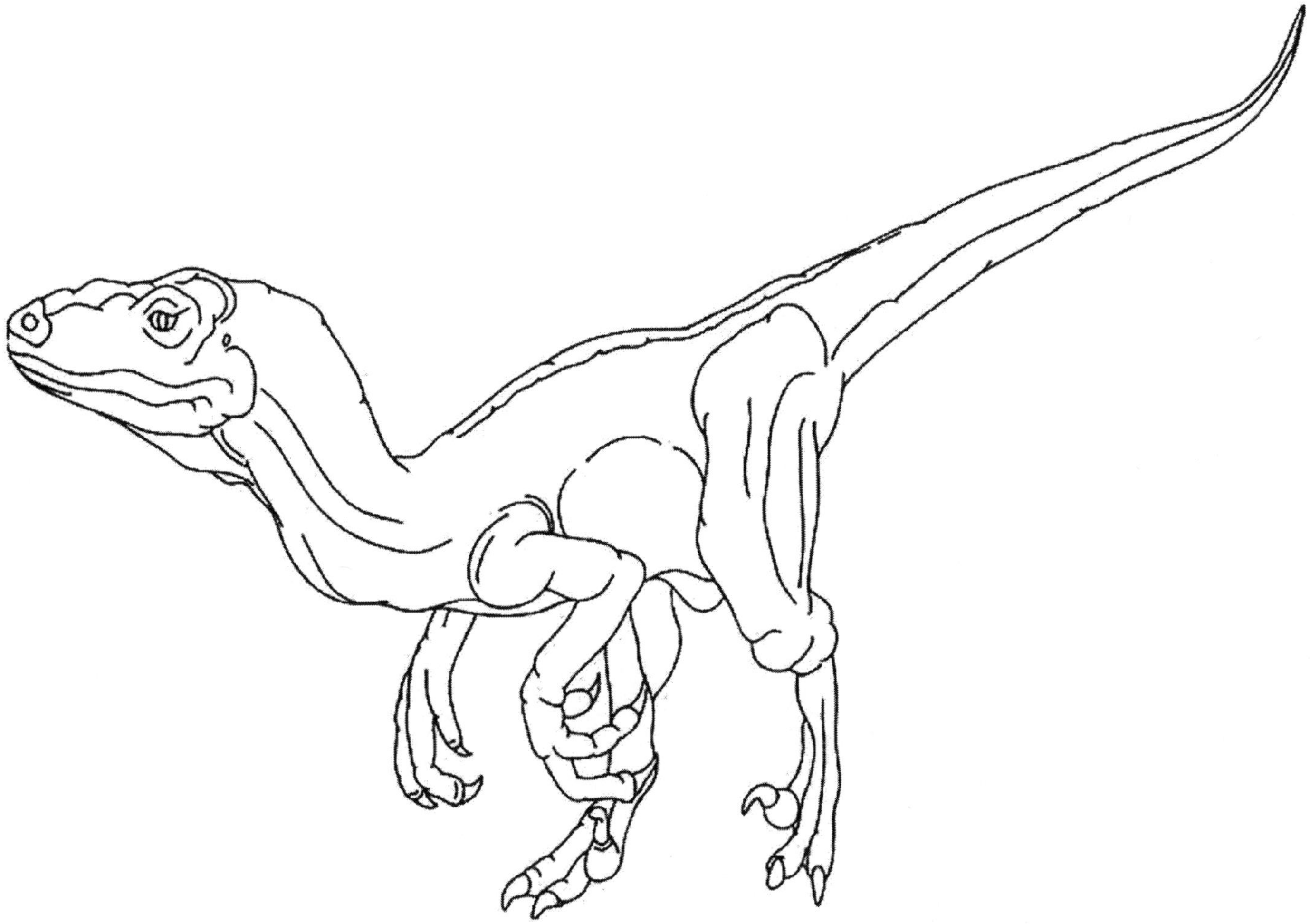

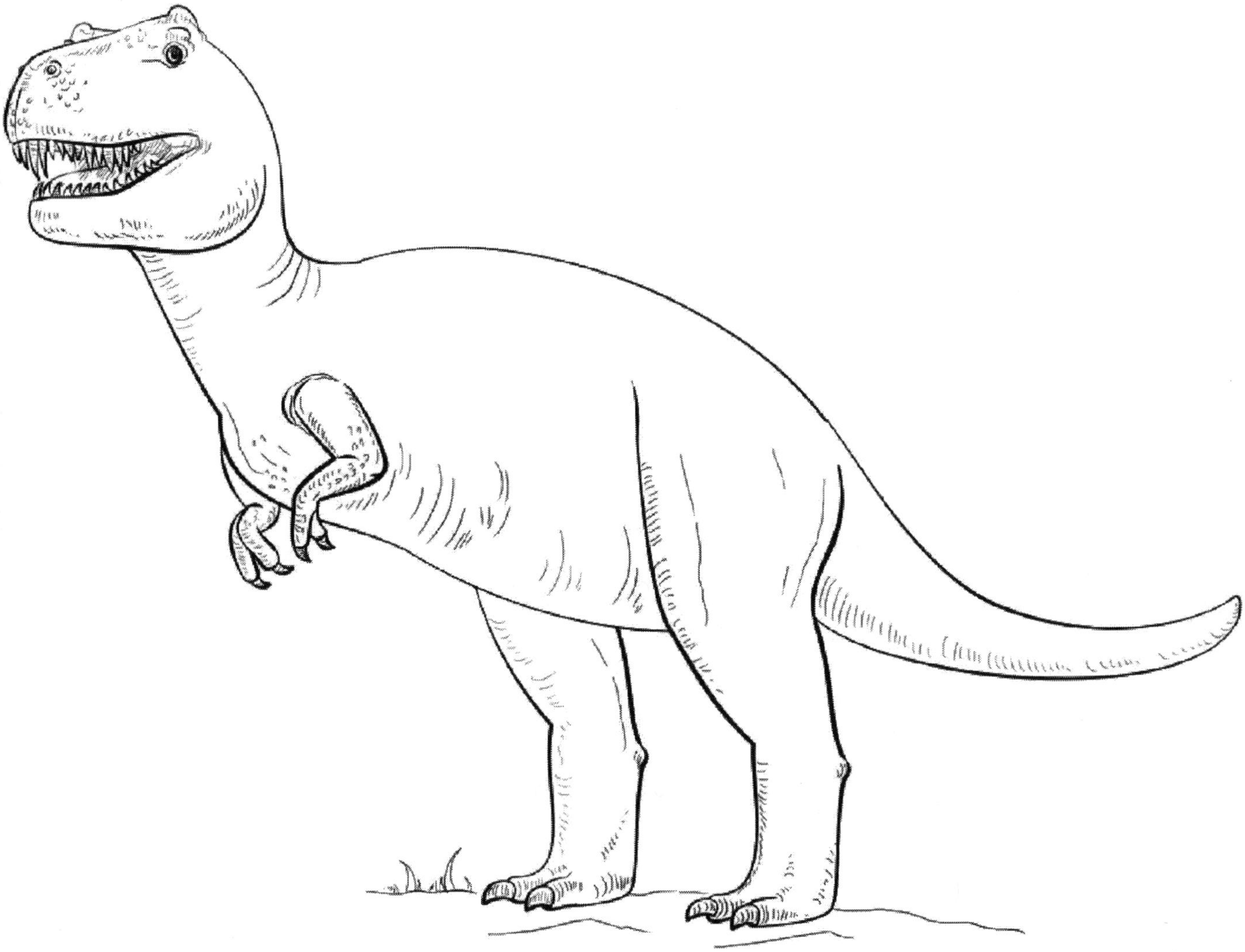

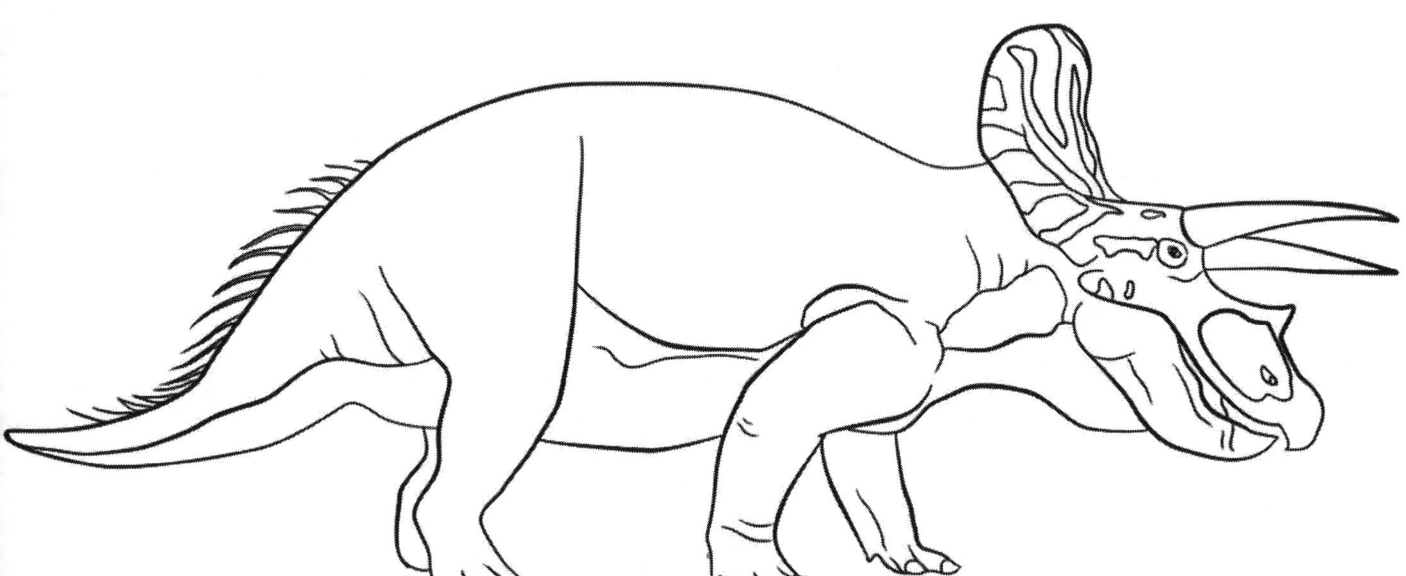

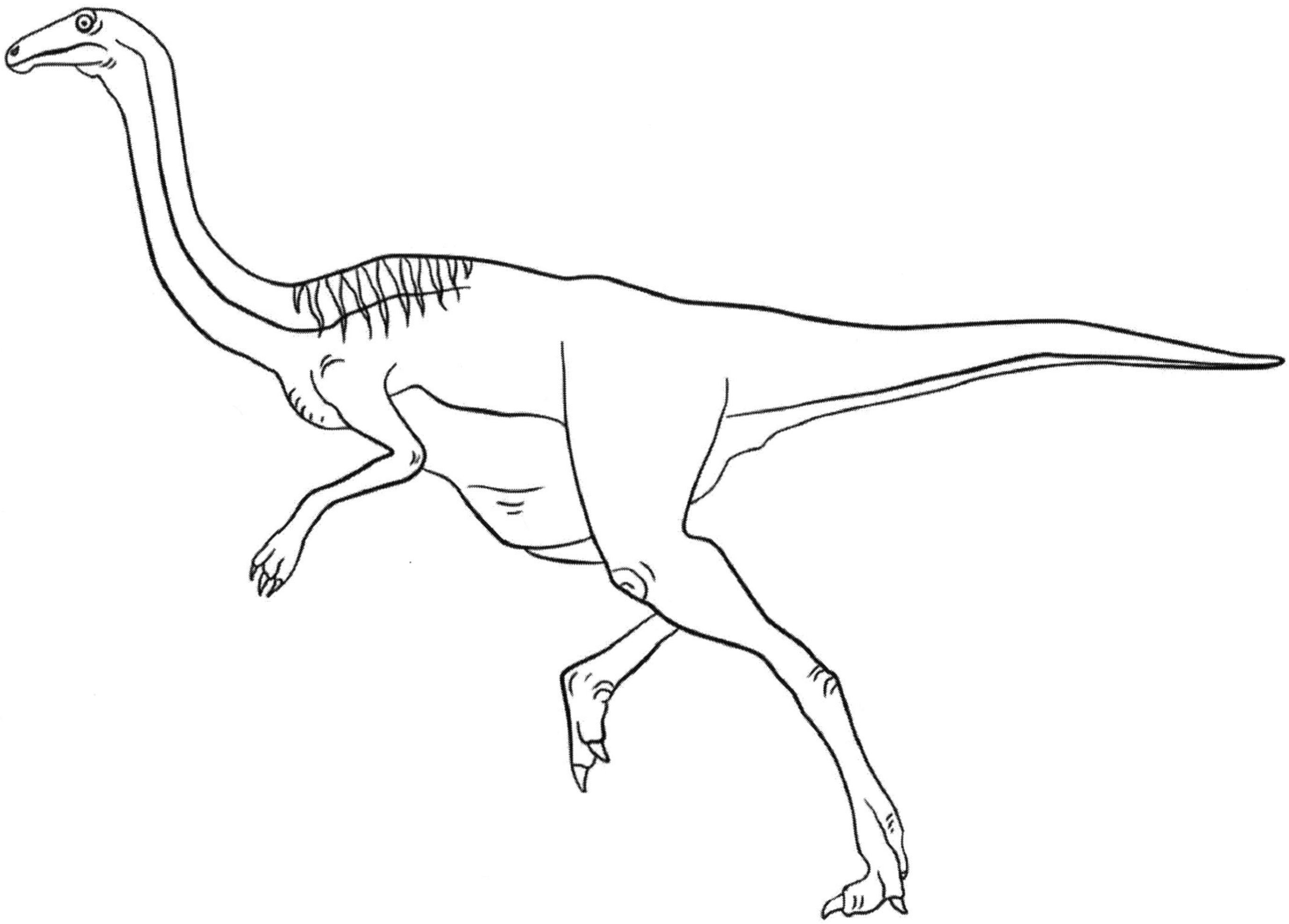

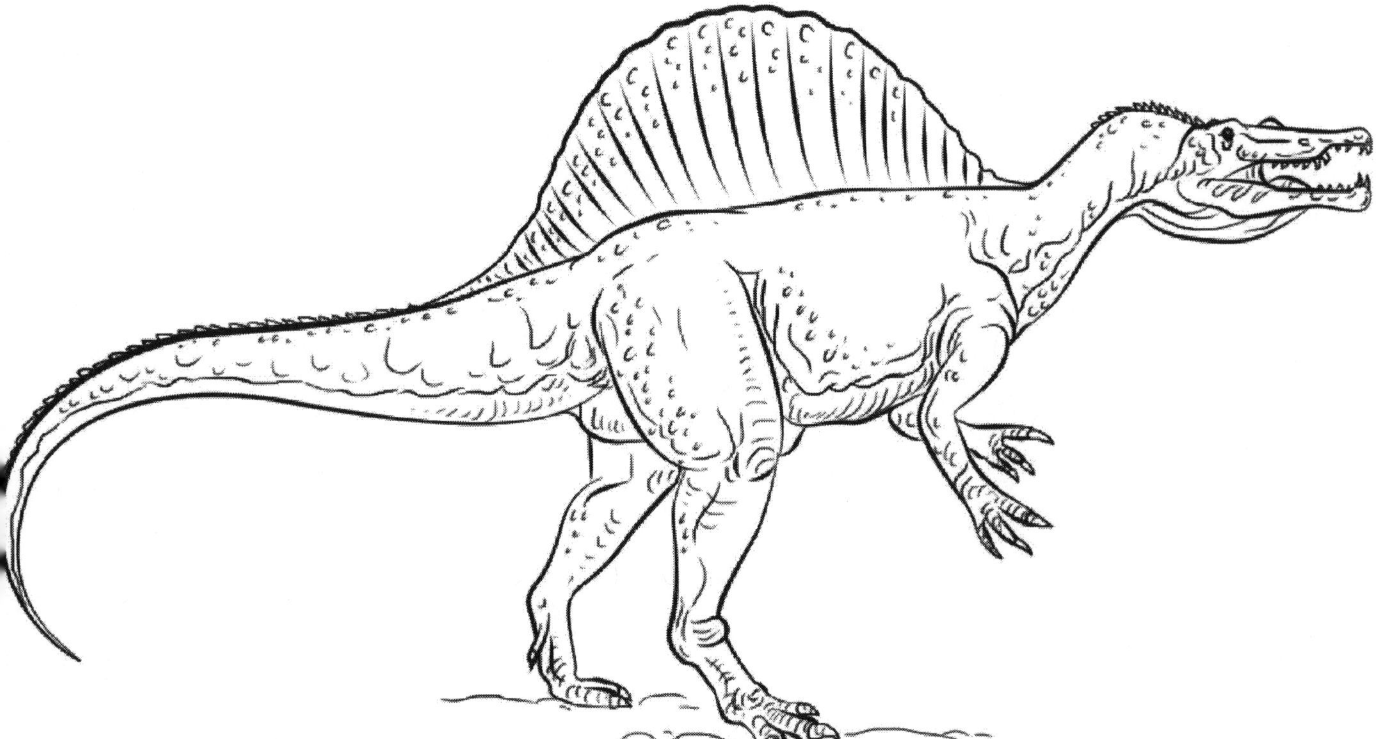

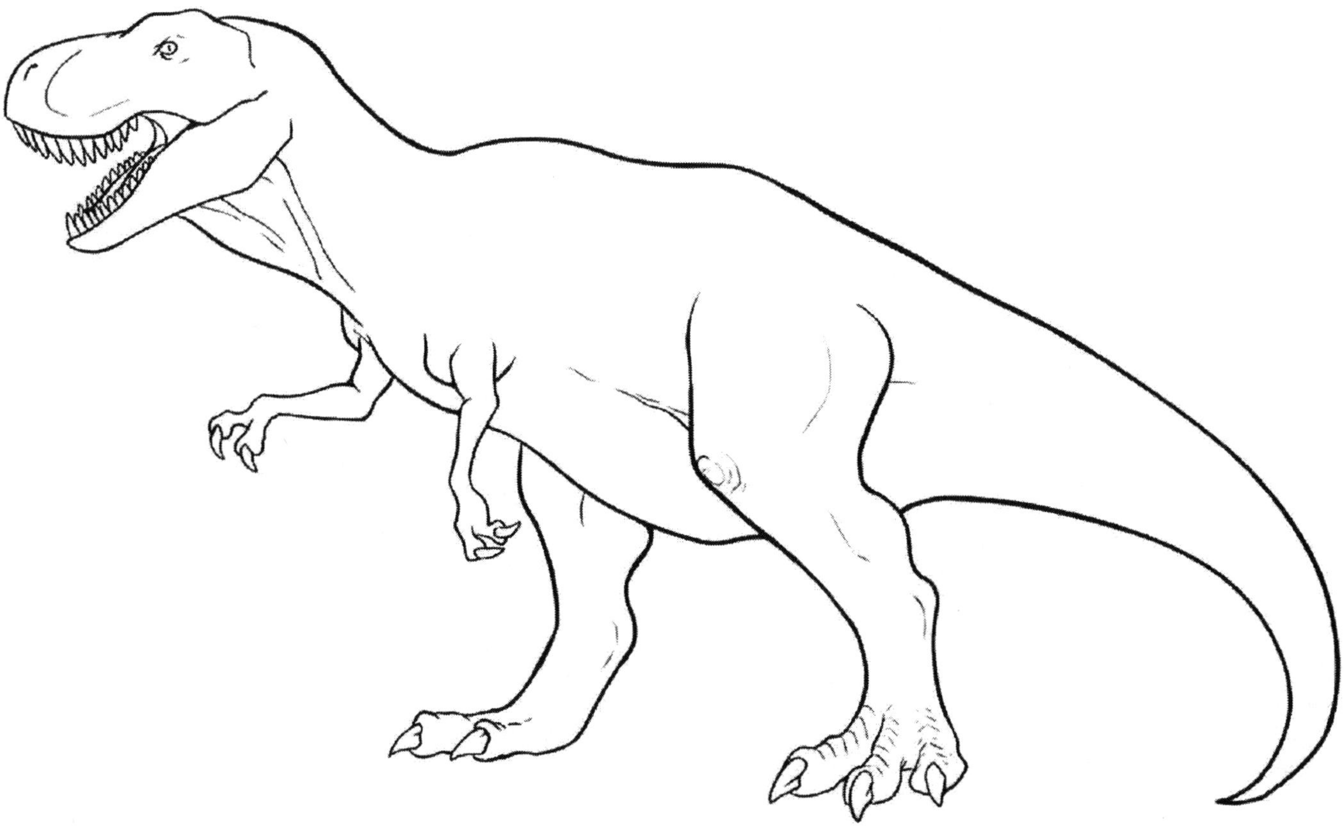

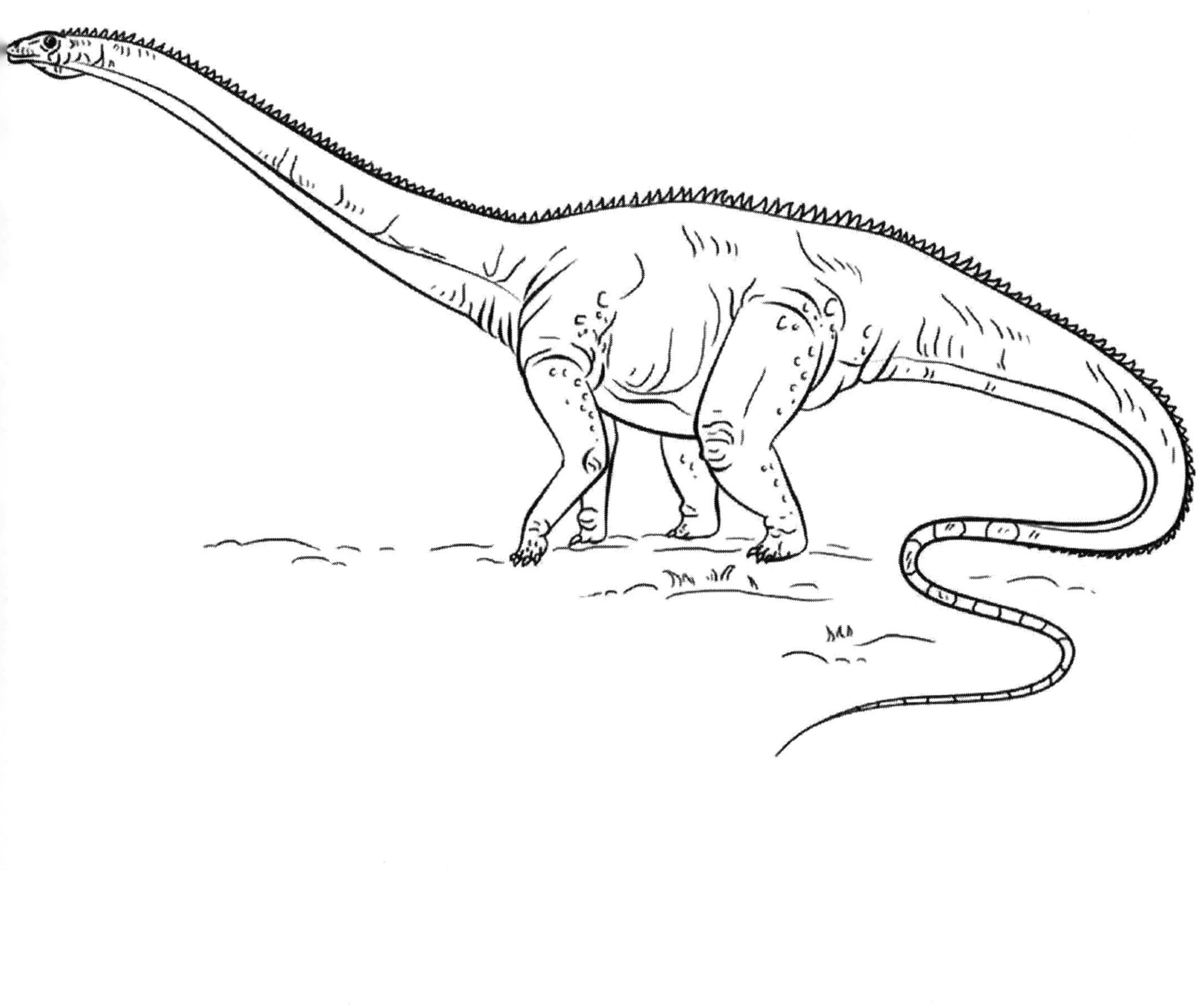

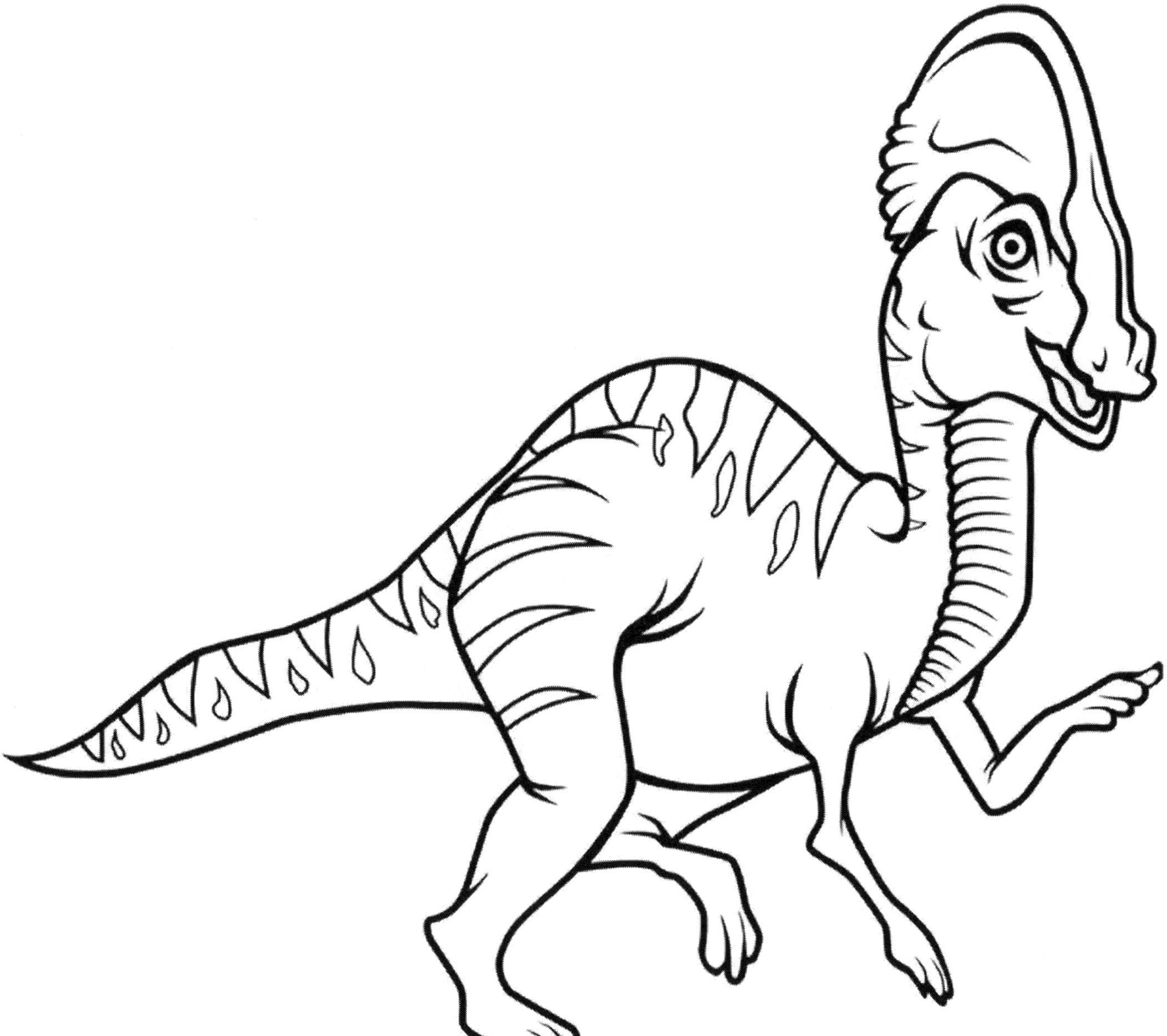

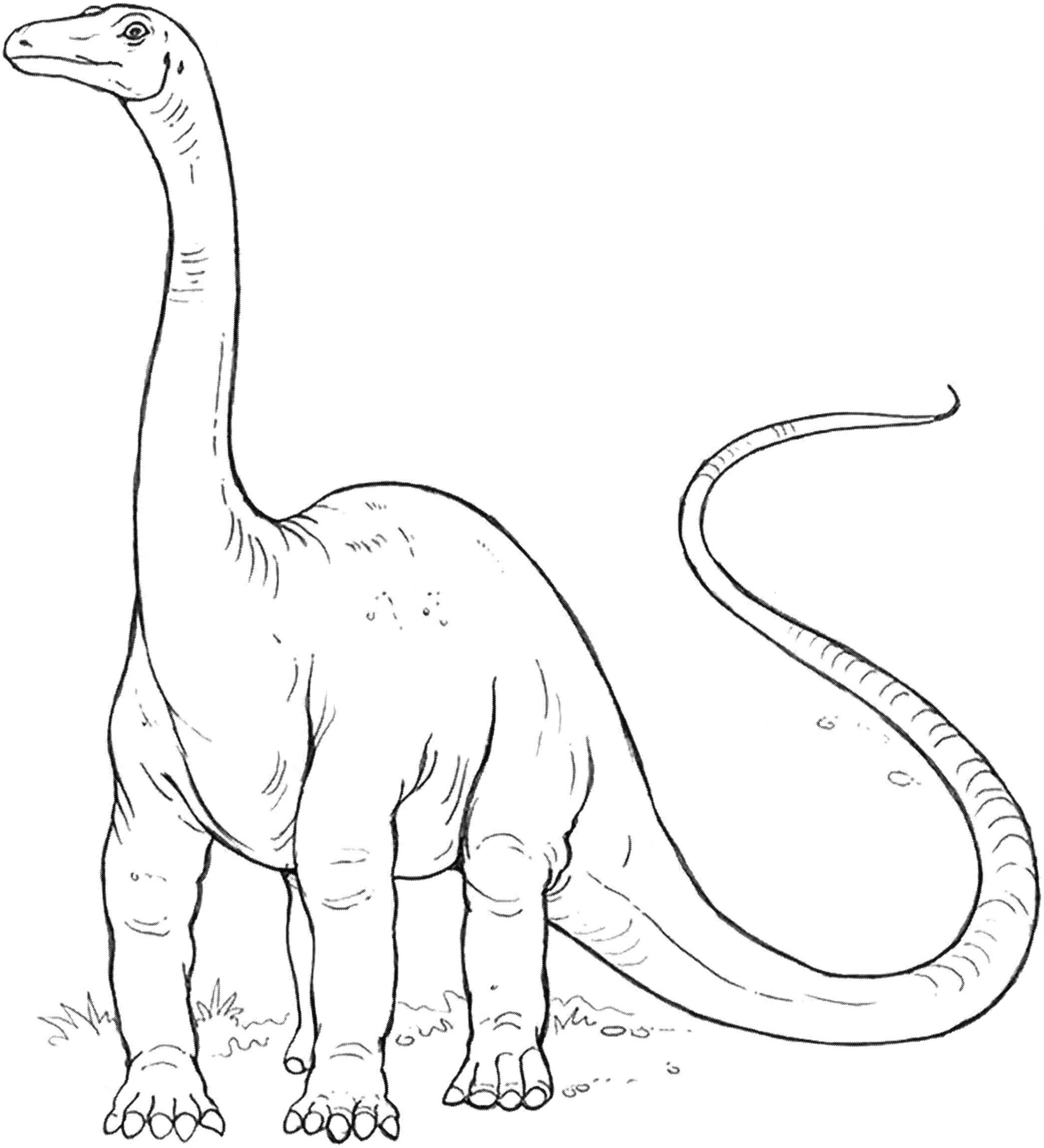

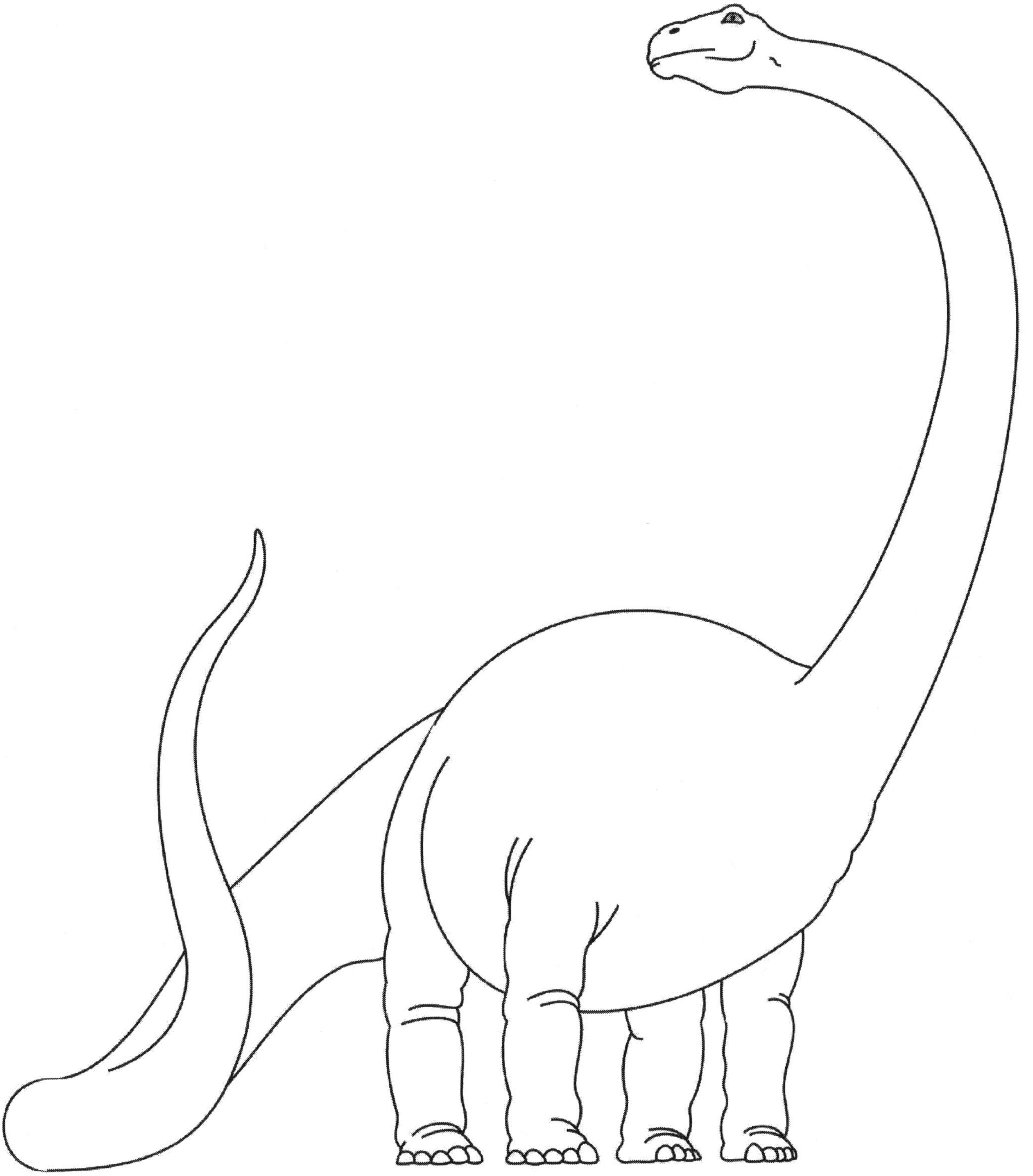

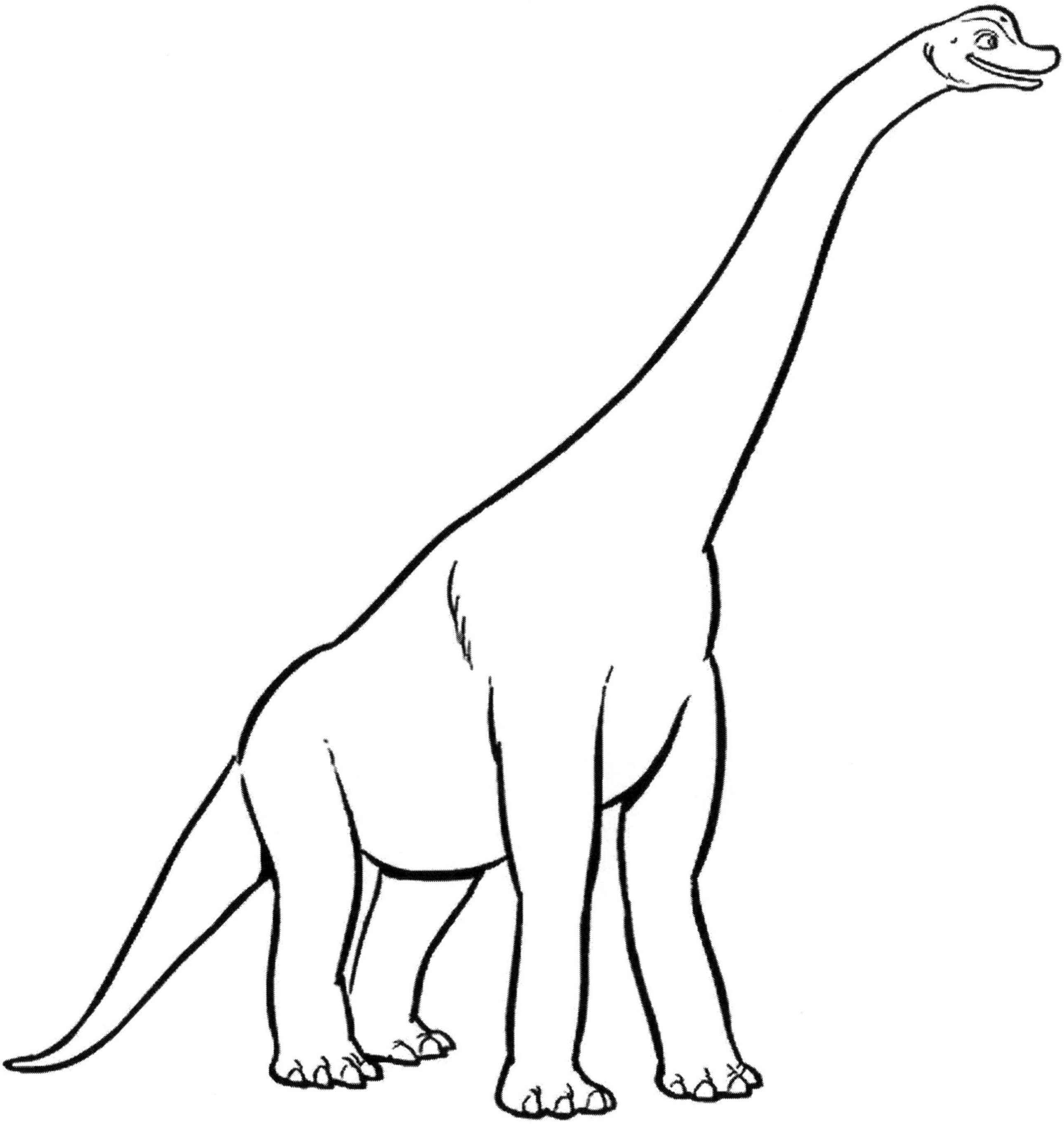

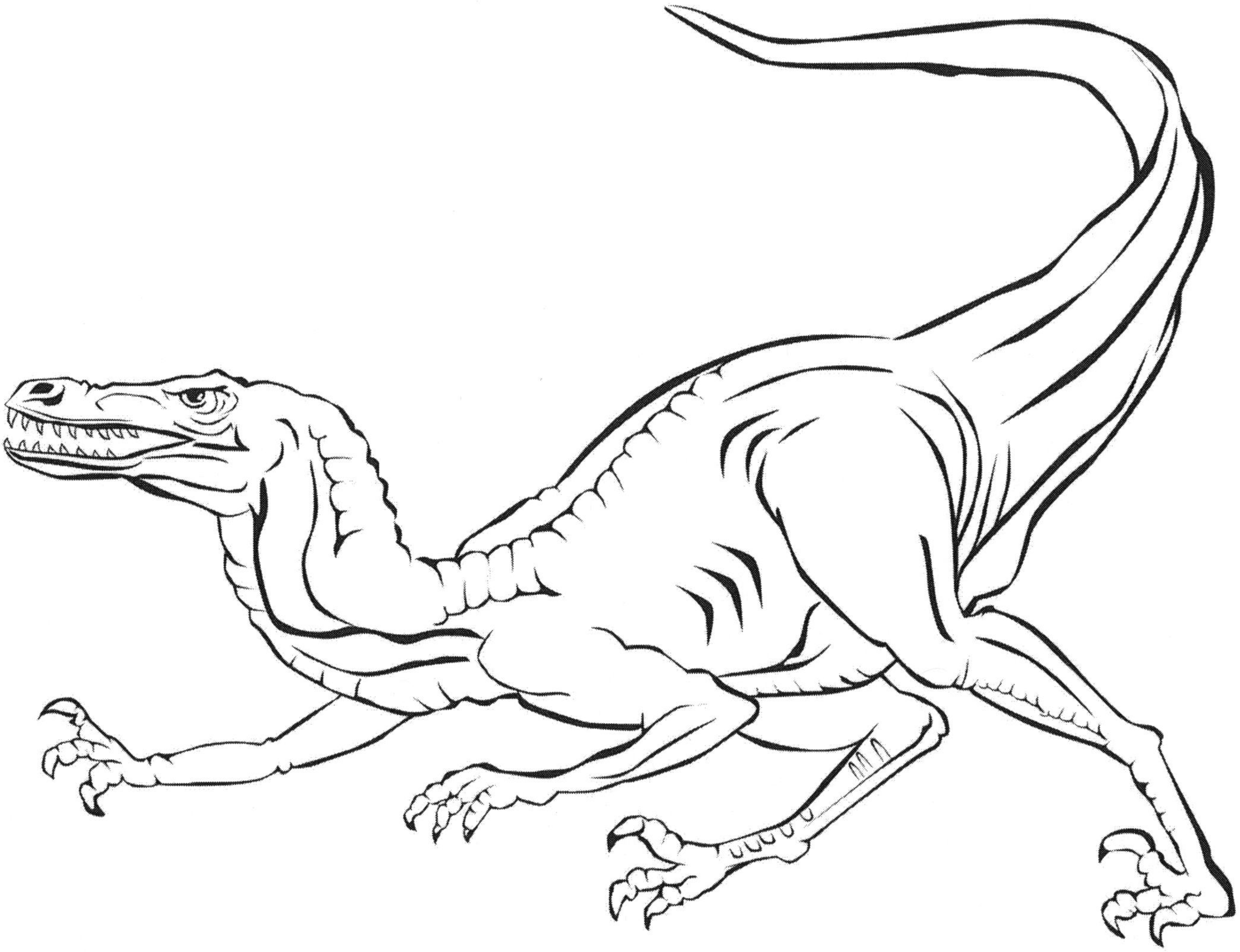

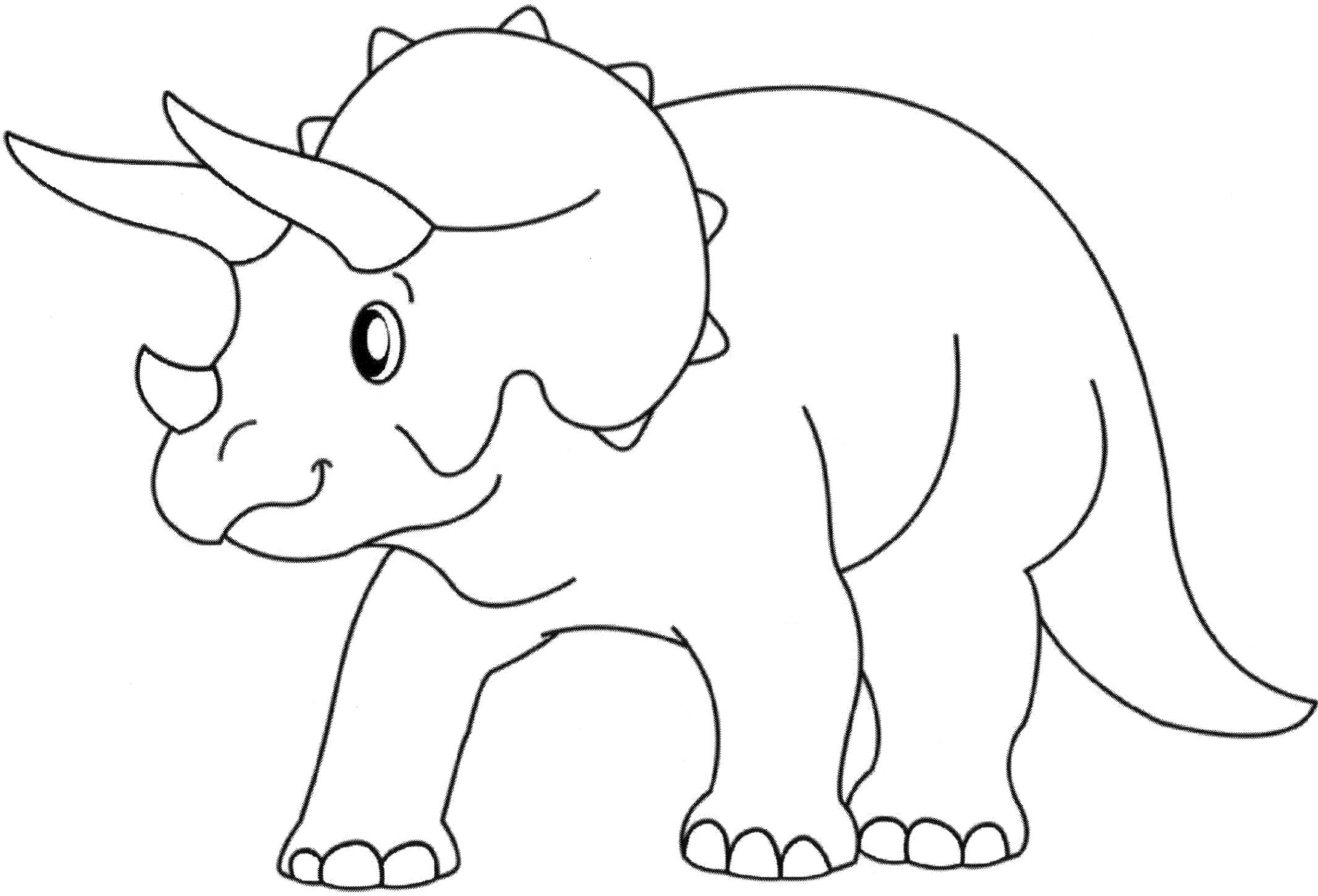

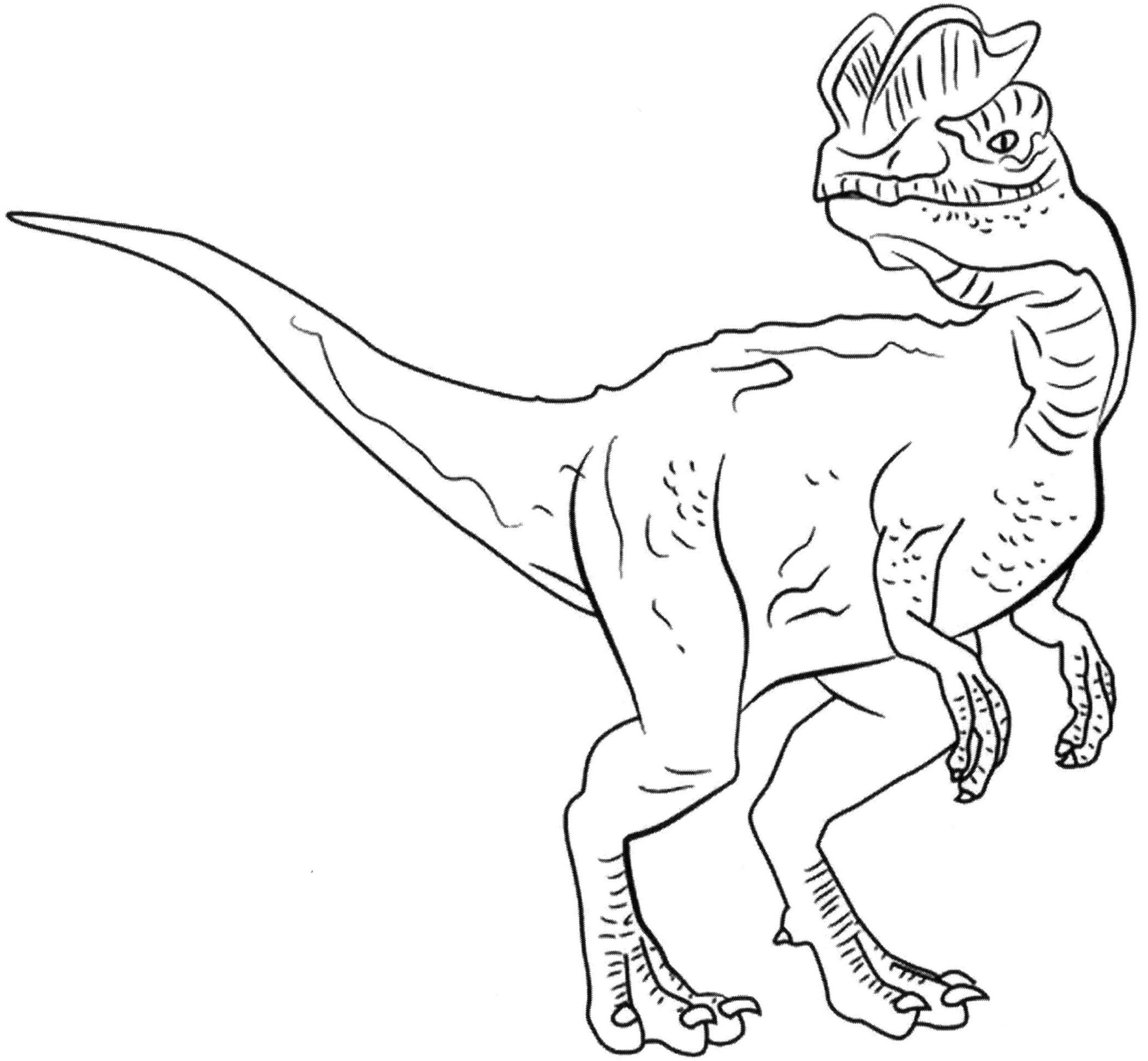

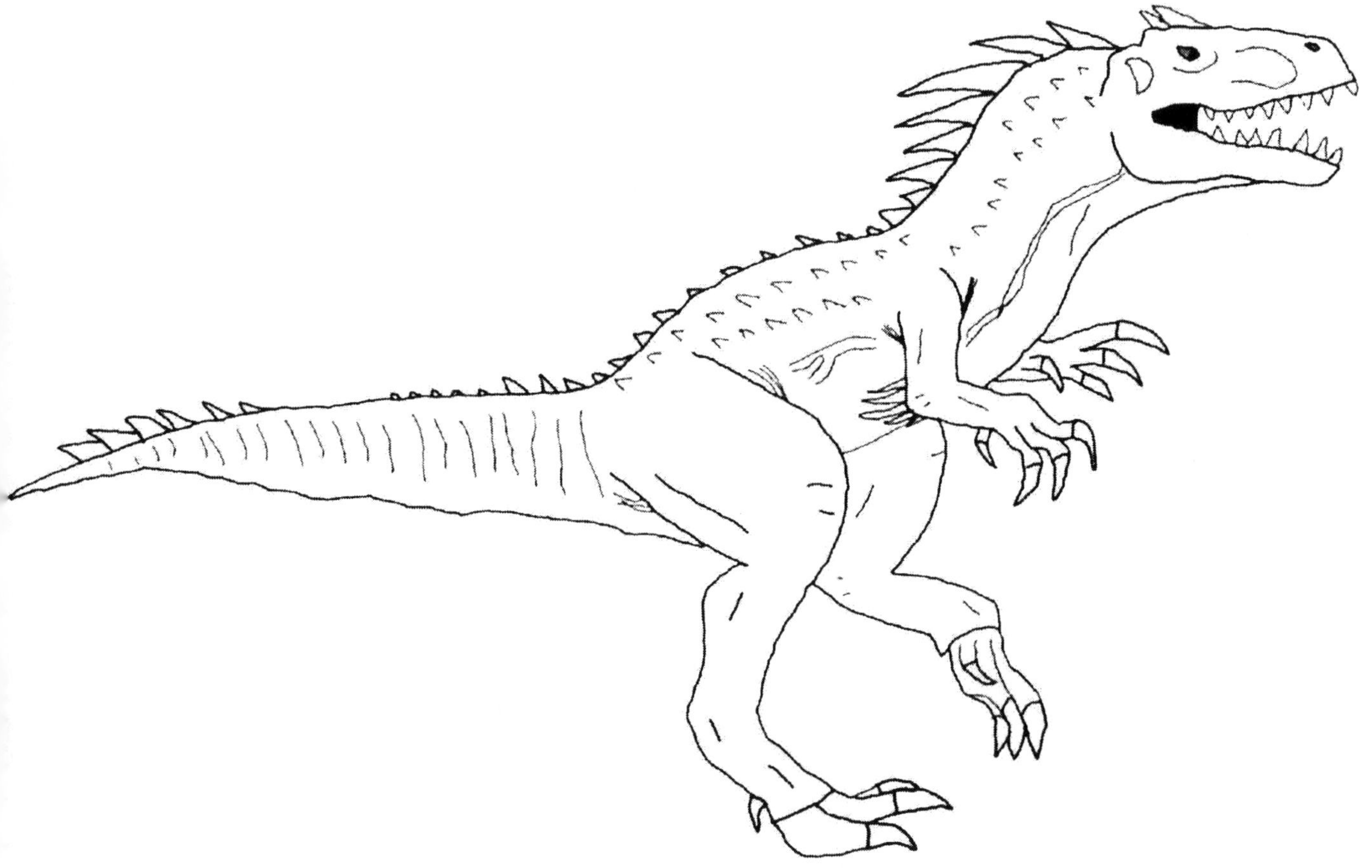

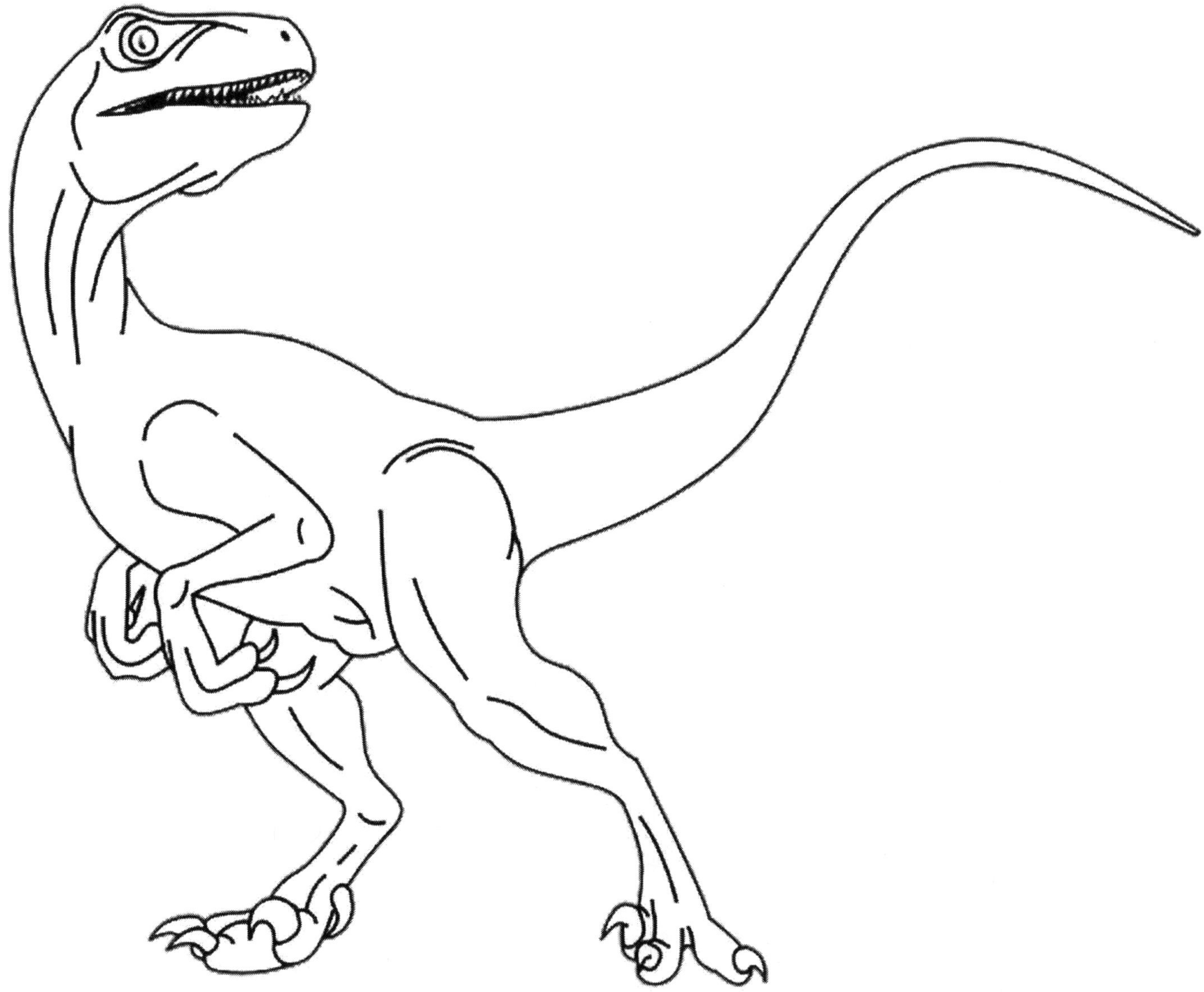

Made in the USA
Monee, IL
07 October 2020

44065103R00072